Race and Crime

Recent Titles in
Bibliographies and Indexes in Ethnic Studies

Annotated Bibliography of Puerto Rican Bibliographies
Fay Fowlie-Flores, compiler

Racism in the United States: A Comprehensive Classified Bibliography
Meyer Weinberg, compiler

Ethnic Periodicals in Contemporary America: An Annotated Guide
Sandra L. Jones Ireland, compiler

Latin American Jewish Studies: An Annotated Guide to the Literature
Judith Laikin Elkin and Ana Lya Sater, compilers

Jewish Alcoholism and Drug Addiction: An Annotated Bibliography
Steven L. Berg, compiler

Guide to Information Resources in Ethnic Museum, Library, and Archival Collections
in the United States
Lois J. Buttlar and Lubomyr R. Wynar, compilers

Racism in Contemporary America
Meyer Weinberg

Race and Crime

An Annotated Bibliography

Compiled by
Katheryn K. Russell, Heather L. Pfeifer,
and Judith L. Jones

Bibliographies and Indexes in Ethnic Studies, Number 8

GREENWOOD PRESS
Westport, Connecticut • London

Library of Congress Cataloging-in-Publication Data

Russell, Katheryn K., 1961–
   Race and crime : an annotated bibliography / compiled by Katheryn K. Russell, Heather L.
Pfeifer, and Judith L. Jones.
      p.   cm.—(Bibliographies and indexes in ethnic studies, ISSN 1046–7882 ; no. 8)
      Includes bibliographical references and index.
      ISBN 0–313–31033–5 (alk. paper)
      1. Crime and race—United States—Bibliography.   I. Pfeifer, Heather L.
II. Jones, Judith L.   III. Title.   IV. Series.
Z5703.5.U5 R87   2000
[HV6197.U5]
016.364'089'00973—dc21   99–088481

British Library Cataloguing in Publication Data is available.

Library of Congress Catalog Card Number: 99–088481
ISBN: 0–313–31033–5
ISSN: 1046–7882

First published in 2000

Greenwood Press, 88 Post Road West, Westport, CT 06881
An imprint of Greenwood Publishing Group, Inc.
www.greenwood.com

Printed in the United States of America

The paper used in this book complies with the
Permanent Paper Standard issued by the National
Information Standards Organization (Z39.48–1984).

10 9 8 7 6 5 4 3 2 1

Dedicated to my students, colleagues, and mentors. - KKR

Man cannot discover new oceans until he has the courage to lose sight of the shore. - Unknown
To my husband, John, and daughters, Emily & Audrey - thank you for being the one constant in this never ending journey and the inspiration that guides me on my voyage. - HLP

I acknowledge all the racial and ethnic minority scholars who have been excluded from criminology and criminal justice literature. - JLJ

Contents

Introduction

In the media, "race and crime" is shorthand for "minorities and crime," and more specifically, "Blacks and crime." This racial reductionism is replicated in the social sciences as well, where explicit studies of "race" are typically studies of Blacks or other minority groups. As a group, Whites have largely been overlooked as criminological subjects. Few studies identify Whites or Whiteness as a basis for evaluating criminal offending. This void contrasts sharply with the deep-well of data and theories on minority criminality. Given that Whites make up approximately two-thirds of arrests each year,[1] they too should be included in any bibliography that purports to encompass "race and crime."

One consequence of using "race and crime" as a referent for "minorities and crime" is that it may unintentionally lend support to genetic explanations of criminal behavior. The failure to examine the relationship between Whiteness and deviance, while at the same time mining the relationship between "minorityness" and deviance, implies that there is something about being a minority that *explains* criminal offending. The genes-race-crime mythology is reinforced by the repeated use of terms such as "Black crime," which have no "White crime" counterpart. This bibliography, then, is both a resource tool for studies on race and crime and a call for more research which reflects the complete racial landscape of criminal offending.

Racial labels aside, however, the annotations chronicled here

---

[1] F.B.I. Uniform Crime Reports, Crime in the United States, 1997. U.S. Department of Justice (1998).

attest to the increasing number of researchers who are focusing their lenses on crime and race. This research, which encompasses a wide-array of disciplines, is not easily accessible. Precious few comprehensive resources exist for someone in search of a race-crime compendium. Four pioneering bibliographies, however, provide a good starting point. First, <u>African American Criminologists, 1970-1996: An Annotated Bibliography</u>,[2] offers the most up-to-date compilation of research by Black criminologists. Lee E. Ross' volume, which includes dissertation abstracts, and book and journal article citations, provides the most complete index to the work product of Black criminologists. Second, <u>Race, Crime and the Criminal Justice System: A Bibliography</u>[3] lists works written about Blacks, Latinos, Native Americans, and Asian Americans, and the criminal justice system. This bibliography indexes material from books, dissertations, journal articles and edited volumes.

Third, Scott Christianson's <u>Index to Minorities & Criminal Justice</u>, offers hundreds of citations for research on minorities and the criminal justice system.[4] Finally, <u>A Comprehensive Bibliography of Criminology and Criminal Justice Literature by Black Authors From 1895-1978</u>, by Helen Taylor-Greene, provides cites for eight decades of research by Black criminologists.[5] Both the Ross and Taylor-Greene bibliographies focus on research by Black scholars, while the other two provide references for literature about minorities. Together, these resources represent ground zero in contemporary research guides for material on minorities and the criminal justice

---

[2] Lee E. Ross. Westport, CT: Greenwood Press, 1998.

[3] <u>Contemporary Social Issues: A Bibliographic Series</u>: No. 45, compiled by Joan Nordquist. Reference and Research Services, 1997.

[4] Scott Christianson. Center on Minorities and Criminal Justice, State University of New York at Albany, 1981.

[5] Helen Taylor-Greene. Hyattsville, MD: Unmah Publications, 1979.

system.[6] Notably, none of these explicitly catalogs literature on Whites and crime.

Building upon these four indexes, this annotated bibliography is a resource guide for those seeking a comprehensive listing of crime and race citations. The work of criminologists, legal scholars, sociologists, biologists, economists, anthropologists, political scientists, politicians, and journalists are represented in this volume. This bibliography is uniquely suited for professors and graduate students who teach courses on crime and race, researchers in search of a detailed guide to race and crime literature, those who seek research on crime related to a particular racial group (e.g., Asian Americans), and those with a general interest who wish to survey the field.

In the final decade of the twentieth century, several national incidents have re-focused our attention on the meaning of race, the meaning of crime, and the sociological consequences of both. Cases involving the spate of shootings at White high-schools, Rodney King/L.A.P.D., O.J. Simpson, Asian American campaign-finance scandals, "Unabomber" Ted Kaczynski, and President Bill Clinton's initiative on race, are some examples. It is our hope that this bibliography will be the beginning of exciting research and reading on crime and race.

---

[6] The editors note that there are other bibliographies that include material on race and crime. They were not included in the above list because their primary focus was not on race and crime research in the U.S. See, e.g., Catherine Matthews and Lesley Lewis, Racism in the Criminal Justice System: A Bibliography. Centre of Criminology, University of Toronto, 1995 (Canadian criminal justice system). Fairchild & Halford, et al. (Eds.), Discrimination and Prejudice: An Annotated Bibliography. Westerfield Enterprises, 1992 (crime and criminal justice system are not the major focus).

Methods

This bibliography includes books, monographs, journal articles, dissertations, special issues, government documents, and websites. The annotations were culled from a variety of databases, including Dissertation Abstracts International, Criminal Justice Abstracts, Sociofile, Psychlit, Social Science Abstracts, OmniSearch-Chicano Database, N.C.J.R.S. (National Criminal Justice Resource Services), LEXIS/NEXIS (law review articles), and VICTOR. Annotation entries include works published from the civil rights era through the final year of the 20th century.[7]

Annotations cover three broad areas: race and offending, race and victimization, and race and criminal justice system professionals (e.g., judges, police officers, and researchers). While there are references to some international studies, most of the citations address the U.S. criminal justice system. By including annotations on criminal justice professionals, we ensure a well-rounded portrait of racial groups and the criminal justice system.

Organization and Other Issues

A. Racial Labels

There are continuing debates about racial labels. For example, which is the appropriate term: Hispanics or Latinos? Blacks or African Americans? American Indians or Native Americans?[8] Often political, these debates revolve around the issue of who -- e.g., group members or outsiders -- determines how a group is called. This

---

[7] Works published through August, 1999 are included.

[8] The authors recognize these as crude racial dichotomies. A variety of terms are used to describe Blacks, including Afro-Americans, African Americans, and Negroes. Likewise, there are many terms used to describe Hispanics, including Chicanos, La Raza, Latinos, and Mexican-Americans.

tension is reflected within racial groups, since members often have competing views on how their group should be labeled. There are no easy answers. A 1995 study conducted by the Bureau of Labor Statistics indicated that "Black," "White," "Hispanic," and "American Indian" were the preferred group labels.[9] In light of these findings, this bibliography uses the following section headings, "Whites," "American Indians," "Asian Americans," "Hispanics" and "African Americans."[10]

Not surprisingly, researchers use a variety of racial labels and categories. As the annotations make clear, many of them reject broad racial labels, opting instead for more precise terms. For example, several entries focus upon racial sub-groups, e.g., Mexican Americans or Korean Americans. Some authors use different racial terms, such as Black and African American, interchangeably. The racial labels used in the annotations are consistent with those used by the researcher--thereby allowing readers to draw their own insights, inferences, and conclusions.

B. Overview

This bibliography is divided into three sections, with nine parts. Section I highlights Race-specific research. Parts 1-5 are devoted to Whites, American Indians, Asian Americans, Hispanics, and African Americans. We begin with the racial groups least studied and end with those most studied. Section II includes General Race Research. Part 6, Multi-Racial, lists research that focuses on two or more racial groups. Part 7 lists Special Issues, Edited Volumes and Guides. These include race and crime publications as part of a series, special issues and bibliographies. Part 8, Government Documents, Reports and Commission Findings, includes studies on race and

---

[9] U.S. Bureau of Labor Statistics, (October, 1995), "A CPS Supplement for Testing Methods of Collecting Racial and Ethnic Information: May, 1995."

[10] "African Americans" was selected over "Blacks" since it is the preferred term for official references.

crime by official bodies. Section III Electronic Resources, Part 9, provides a listing of World Wide Web citations for government documents on crime and justice.[11] Each annotation provides a complete citation[12] and brief summary which includes the racial group of interest, research methods and conclusions.

---

[11] With the substantial number of criminal justice web-sites presently accessible via the internet, a determination as to which sites to include were made based on the following criteria: the site provided a vast array of information either directly or indirectly (via links); it was well-organized and 'user-friendly' in its presentation; it provided links to other related resource or provided a search tool that enabled the user to perform word/topic searches.

[12] In the few instances where an author's first name could not be determined, the first initial is provided.

I

RACE-SPECIFIC RESEARCH

Part 1

Whites

Anderson, Craig, & Kathryn Anderson. (1996). Violent crime rate studies in a philosophical context: A destructive testing approach to heat and Southern culture of violence effects. Journal of Personality and Social Psychology, 70 (4), 740-756.

Article reports findings from two studies which offer an empirical assessment of the role temperature and Southern culture play in the prediction of violence. Data based on U.S. cities in 1980. Authors use a destructive testing approach. The first study analyzes the effect of heat on violent crime rates and the second focuses on violent crime arrest rates among Whites. The studies indicate that temperature and rates of violence are highly correlated.

Bushway, Shawn D. (1998). The impact of an arrest on the job stability of young White American men. Journal of Research in Crime and Delinquency, 35 (4), 454-479.

Study examines the effect of arrest on employment of White men by testing whether employment instability among criminals is due to lack of social and human capital necessary to succeed or whether employers avoid hiring individuals who will not succeed in the labor market. Data includes 178

White men in the workforce from 1983 to 1986, drawn from two waves of National Youth Survey. Using job length measures, study found that formal contact with the criminal justice system, rather than criminal activity, damages job prospects. Using job stability measure, it was determined that neither offending nor arrest had impact on job stability.

Delgado, Richard. (1994). Rodrigo's eighth chronicle: Black crime, White fears -- On the social construction of threat. Virginia Law Review, 80 (2), 503-548.

The author discusses several race and crime topics, including White crime. He explores why and how the study of White crime has been neglected. Analysis includes a consideration of the language of crime and deviance. Further, Delgado details the prevalence and costs of White crime, such as white-collar crime and corporate offending. He concludes that White crime is significantly more costly than Black crime.

Feagin, Joe R., & Vera Hernan. (1995). White racism. New York: Routledge.

Wide-ranging discussion and analysis of the impact of White racism on American society and in particular, Black life. Through a series of case studies, authors evaluate the costs of racism. In area of criminal law, text details racial hoaxes and police brutality. Authors conclude that White racism has material, moral, and psychological costs for Whites as well as Blacks.

Fox, James Alan, & Jack Levin. (1998). Multiple homicide: Patterns of serial and mass murder. In Michael Tonry (Ed.), Crime and justice: A review of research: Vol.23 (pp.407-455). Chicago: University of Chicago Press.

Review examines research about multiple homicide such as

serial and mass murder. The typical serial killer is a White male in his late 20s or 30s who targets strangers encountered near his work or home. They tend to be sociopaths who satisfy personal needs by killing. Contrastly, the mass murderer deliberately and methodically kills people who he knows well, using a firearm. Both serial killer and mass murderer have same motivational typology: power, revenge, loyalty, profit, and terror.

Gordon, Randall, Jennifer Michels, & Caroline Nelson. (1996). Majority group perceptions of criminal behavior: The accuracy of race-related crime stereotypes. Journal of Applied Social Psychology, 26 (2), 148-159.

Study explores Whites' perceptions of the relative frequency of crimes committed by various racial and ethnic groups. Data include results of questionnaires completed by a sample of 224 students attending a small Midwestern university, which were then compared with the 1992 U.C.R. data. Whites rank white-collar crimes as more commonly committed by Whites and rank aggravated assault and motor vehicle theft as more commonly committed by Blacks. Findings indicate that Whites underestimate the number of blue-collar and violent crimes committed by Whites and overestimate the number of white-collar crimes committed by Whites.

Groh, Thomas. (1976). A preliminary study of patient characteristics in a correctional setting. Corrective and Social Psychiatry and Journal of Behavior Technology Methods and Therapy, 22 (1), 21-23.

Research examines characteristics of inmates in therapy to determine whether treatment groups are the result of random or discriminatory selection. Author hypothesized that inmates chosen for therapy would tend to be White, have higher I.Q. and educational backgrounds, and prior treatment history.

Data were collected from an unnamed MidWestern medium-security institution.   Analysis found support for the hypothesis.

Gross, Ariela. (1998). Litigating Whiteness: Trials of racial determination in the nineteenth-century South. <u>Yale Law Journal, 108</u> (1), 109-185.

A legal analysis of how "Whiteness" was defined by Southern U.S. courts in the nineteenth century. Author reviews the types of evidence courts considered, including an exploration of the prevailing sociological and scientific ideologies of race and racial classification, and racial "performance." Analysis is based upon review of 68 cases of racial determination appealed to state supreme courts in the 1900s South. These legal appeals typically involve Blacks who have been charged with a crime because of their race or who were denied an entitlement (e.g., inheritance) because of their race.

Hagen, Michael G. (1995). References to racial issues. <u>Political Behavior, 17</u> (1), 49-88.

Article explores the readiness with which issues of race come to the minds of Americans. This is measured by the frequency with which they refer to racial issues when discussing politics. The author examines the possibility that a language of symbolic racism has taken the place of socially unacceptable explicit references to race among Whites. Findings are based on national election surveys from 1952-1992. Research indicates that crime, poverty, and welfare have become code words for Whites to communicate anxiety about race.

Hamm, Mark. (1993). <u>American Skinheads: The criminology and control of hate crime</u>. Westport, CT: Praeger.

Ethnographic study examines the spread of a modern form of

Nazism by White youths. The research indicates that Skinheads advocate a Neo-Nazi ideology that views the self-respect, power, and economic wealth of working class Whites as threatened by racial and ethnic minorities. The author recommends the boycott of "White power" rock music, litigation against publishers of White racist literature, stricter gun control legislation, the removal of sensationalism in media coverage of domestic terrorism, and more research on the etiology of domestic terrorism.

Hurwitz, Jon, & Mark Peffley. (1997). Public perceptions of race and crime: The role of racial stereotypes. American Journal of Political Science, 41 (2), 375-401.

Analysis of Whites' stereotypes of Blacks in the context of crime. The sample includes 501 adults in the Lexington, Kentucky area, based upon a 1994 telephone survey. The findings indicate a strong relationship between the images Whites have of Blacks and their judgements of how violent Black offenders should be punished.

Lester, David. (1995). Serial killers: The insatiable passion. Philadelphia: Charles Press Publishers.

Author explores the common characteristics that serial murderers have in common, their reasons for killing, the frequency of serial murders in the United States, and the public's concern over these types of murders. Research establishes that almost all serial killers in modern times have been White. Further, very few serial killers use firearms to kill their victims. Because there are many types of serial murderers, the author concludes that it is difficult to construct a single profile.

Meyers, John C. (1973). Marijuana use by White college students. Crime and Delinquency, 19 (1), 79-90.

Study examines marijuana use among White college students to develop a typology of marijuana users. Using data drawn from 300 White marijuana users from a large Eastern university, study found that there are a growing number of White middle-class college marijuana users. Responsibility-coping and social adjustment were two suggested factors that may have contributed to marijuana use by this group. Treatment based on this typology may benefit offenders and probation service.

Miller, Walter B. (1969). White gangs. Transaction, 6 (10), 11-26.

Analysis of two White gangs in Midcity, a lower-class section of a large city in which a ten-year study (1954-1964) was conducted. Research found that the average major gang numbered 150 boys and 40 girls, ranging from 12 to 21 years old. For the whole community, 64 percent of the boys and 18 percent of the girls hung out at the local corner. For many, the gang was their whole life. The gang was an ordered and adaptive form of association with rational members. Gangs serve as an instrument to impart knowledge about value of individual competence, limitations of law-violating behavior, uses and abuses of authority, and skills of interpersonal relations.

Moore, Jack. (1993). Skinheads shaved for battle: A cultural history of American Skinheads. Bowling Green, OH: Bowling Green State University Popular Press.

Text, based upon interviews with Skinhead youth, investigates the English roots of the U.S. Skinhead movement. Since the mid-1980s, Skinhead brutality has been directed toward gays, Jews, Latinos, and Blacks. Author concludes that the Skinhead subculture provides youth with an immediate and distinct identity, and a sense of belonging to a community.

Peffley, Mark, Jon Hurwitz, & Paul M. Sniderman. (1997). Racial stereotypes and Whites' political views of Blacks in the context of welfare and crime. American Journal of Political Science, 41 (1), 30-60.

Study uses multiple regression to examine Whites' negative stereotypes of Blacks in the context of welfare and crime. The study is based on the 1991 Race and Politics Survey administered by the Survey Research Center at the University of California at Berkeley. Sample includes 2,223 Whites. Findings show that Whites holding negative stereotypes are substantially more likely to judge Blacks more harshly than similarly described Whites, in relation to welfare and crime policy. However, Whites with negative perceptions of Blacks respond favorably to Blacks when confronted with information that clearly contradicts their stereotype.

Pendleton, Michael R. (1996). Crime, criminals and guns in 'natural settings': Exploring the basis for disarming federal rangers. American Journal of Police, 15 (4), 3-26.

Research evaluates crime in U.S. federal forests and parks. Data were drawn from 1992 and 1994 in a single national forest and park, located in a Western state. The typical offender was a 30-year-old White male. A small number of offenders account for the majority of crimes. Environmental offenses and theft were the most frequent crimes reported.

Phillips, G. Howard. (1976). Rural crimes and rural offenders. Columbus, OH: Ohio State University Agricultural Economics and Rural Sociology Department.

Study examines rural crimes which are offenses commited in an area with a population of 2,500 or less. Data were drawn from Uniform Crime Reports and two studies on rural crime and Ohio rural crime from 1965 through 1974. Study found that most rural offenders were under 30 years old (74 percent), male (87 percent), and urban residents (60 percent). Ninety-three percent of the rural offenders were White.

Pinkney, Alphonso. (1994). White hate crimes: Howard Beach and other racial atrocities. Chicago: Third World Press.

Pinkney details seven White hate crimes which occurred in New York in the 1980s and 1990s. Several cases are discussed including Eleanor Bumpers, Bernhard Goetz, Michael Griffith, Yusuf Hawkins, and Michael Stewart. Author provides a socio-political context for evaluating causes and reactions to White-on-Black crime. He also reports on issues related to anti-Black violence, including police brutality.

Roebuck, Julian, & Komanduri Murty. (1996). The Southern subculture of drinking and driving: A generalized deviance model for the Southern White male. New York: Garland.

Study analyzes the history of 311 White males with Driving Under the Influence (D.U.I.) convictions. Ninety percent of the sample had prior convictions. Authors posit that recidivistic behavior is the result of subcultural interaction. The most dangerous group of recidivists were those offenders who had a lengthier and more serious arrest history and criminal lifestyle.

Sapp, Allen, Timothy Huff, & Gary Gordon. (1994). A report of essential findings from a study of serial arsonists. Quantico, VA: National Center for the Analysis of Violent Crime, U.S. F.B.I. Academy.

Study examines U.S. serial arsonists housed in prisons, jails, and mental health facilities. Data were drawn from audio and video-taped interviews and case studies. Those in the first sample (42) were interviewed between 1978-1980. Those in the second group (41) were interviewed between 1990-1992.

Findings indicate that the average arsonist is a White male, twenty seven years old, and poorly educated. An average of 31 fires were set by offenders in the sample.

Skogan, Wesley G. (1995). Crime and racial fears of White Americans. Annals of the American Academy of Political and Social Science, 539, 59-71.

Survey studies confirm that residential proximity to Blacks is related to White fear of crime, and that Whites who are prejudiced are more fearful. The fear-provoking effects of proximity and prejudice are independent; however, Whites currently living closer to Blacks register lower levels of prejudice than do those who live farther away. Author suggests that this may be due to the ability of Whites to use segregated housing markets to distance themselves from minority neighborhoods.

St. John, Craig, & Tamara Heald-Moore. (1996). Age, racial prejudice and fear of criminal victimization in public settings. Sociological Focus, 29 (1), 15-31.

The authors examine the extent to which anti-Black prejudice influences the positive relationship between age and fear of criminal victimization in public settings among Whites. Analysis was based on data from the 1993 Oklahoma City Survey of 416 adults. Researchers found that higher levels of racial prejudice among elderly Whites affected fear of crime.

Tolnay, Stewart E., & E. M. Beck. (1995). A festival of violence: An analysis of Southern lynchings, 1882-1930. Chicago: University of Illinois Press.

Authors report that between 1882 and 1930, almost 2,500 African Americans were victims of lynching in ten Southern states. This statistic does not include casualties of urban race riots, the victims of racially-motivated murders by a single killer, or the countless other beatings, whippings or assaults suffered by Blacks. Utilizing a comparative method, the authors examine temporal and geographical patterns of lynchings during this time period. Further, they consider various theoretical explanations for lynching.

Warren, Janet I., Robert R. Hazelwood, & Park E. Dietz. (1996). Sexually sadistic serial killer. Journal of Forensic Sciences, 41 (6), 970-974.

Study explores the characteristics and the crime scene behavior of 20 sexually sadistic serial murderers. Data were complied from case files obtained by the F.B. I. National Center of the Analysis of Violent Crime. Findings show that this group shares similarities across demographic, region, offense behavior, and victim acquisition techniques. Ninety-five percent of the subjects were White. Research indicates that these offenders carefully planned their crimes and most kidnapped their victims. Predators also inflicted a variety of painful sexual acts and torture on their victims, and resorted to either strangulation or stabbing when killing them.

Wooden, Wayne. (1995). Renegade kids, suburban outlaws: From youth culture to delinquency. Belmont, CA: Wadsworth.

Based on case studies and interviews conducted with teenagers from suburban California. The author distinguishes between "Renegade kids," those who are relatively harmless identity seekers immersed in the constantly changing youth styles and cultures, and the "Suburban outlaws," those who are non-conformist rebels prone to law-breaking. Suburban outlaws committed law-violating acts and embraced more deviant identities. Questionnaires completed by racist Skinhead group members evidenced hatred against minorities. The author indicates that youths with a history of anti-social behavior, especially bullying, are more likely to become teenage Skinheads.

Young, Thomas J. (1990). Violent hate groups in rural America. International Journal of Offender Therapy and Comparative Criminology, 34 (1), 15-21.

Article examines criminal activities of hate groups throughout the American farm belt from a social, political, and economic perspective of rural life. Author traces the evolution of the hate group movement from the Ku Klux Klan to the Neo-Nazis. While Young recognizes there are differences between these groups, a commonality is their adherence to the "Identity Movement," which asserts that White Anglo-Saxons are God's chosen people and America their promised land.

Part 2

American Indians

Alvarez, Alexander, & Ronet Bachman. (1996). American Indians and sentencing disparity: An American test. Journal of Criminal Justice, 24 (6), 549-561.

Article examines sentencing disparities between American Indian and White inmates. Data from the active inmate population incarcerated in Arizona state correctional facilities in May, 1990. Regression analysis is used to predict the sentences received by the two groups convicted of homicide, sexual assault, robbery, assault, burglary, or larceny. After controlling for prior felony record and other demographic variables, authors found American Indians received longer sentences for robbery and burglary than White inmates convicted of same offense. In cases of homicide, however, Whites received significantly longer sentences than their American Indian counterparts. Authors discuss findings in the context of various theoretical arguments.

Bachman, Ronet. (1991). An analysis of American Indian homicide: A test of social disorganization and economic deprivation at the reservation county level. Journal of Research in Crime and Delinquency, 28 (4), 456-472.

Although homicide rates among the American Indian

population are documented to be double that of the White population, criminologists have devoted little attention to examining its etiology. Presenting a multi-variate analysis of American Indian homicide at the reservation county level, this study tests indicators of social disorganization and economic deprivation, while controlling for other demographic variables. Results indicate that both factors contribute to high levels of lethal violence in reservation communities.

Bachman, Ronet, & Murray A. Strauss. (1992). Death and violence on the reservation: Homicide, family violence, and suicide in American Indian populations. Westport, CT: Auburn House.

Using personal narratives to illustrate statistical data, text attempts to locate the causes of violence in American Indian populations. Comparisons are made between national and regional patterns of American Indian, White, and Black homicide rates, as well as suicide rates for all three ethnic groups. Alternative explanations for such trends are discussed, including the discriminatory practices by the judicial system and the meager medical resources available in American Indian communities.

Barker, Michael Lynn. (1994). American Indian tribal police: An overview and case-study (Doctoral dissertation, State University of New York at Albany, 1994). Dissertation Abstracts International, 56 (1), 365.

Research explores the development of American Indian tribal police. Specifically, how tribal police have come to incorporate Anglo-Saxon professional ideals which have ultimately worked to increase existing mechanisms of social control. Author finds that a continuum has emerged by which tribal police have slowly evolved from an American Indian-based model to the current Anglo-Saxon professional model. The legal and jurisdictional environment in which this charge occurred is also discussed.

Benge, W. B. (1960). Law and order on Indian reservations. <u>Federal Bar Journal, 20</u> (3), 223-229.

Article examines the development of tribal law beginning with the 1832 decision, *Worcester v. Georgia*. Analysis extends through the contemporary tribal justice system which is patterned after an Anglo model of jurisprudence. Author presents detailed discussion of two parallel branches operating in the current tribal justice system -- the tribal court and the court of Indian offenses. Author also discusses federal legislation which pertains to jurisdictional issues.

Bond-Maupin, Lisa Jane. (1992). American Indians, imposed law and self-determination: Juvenile justice in Gila River Indian community (Doctoral dissertation, Arizona State University, 1992). <u>Dissertation Abstracts International, 54</u> (2), 689.

Dissertation examines the development of federal Indian policy, the role of the Bureau of Indian Affairs, and the transformation of indigenous systems of law and government in Indian communities. This overview and analysis is combined with literature on American Indian crime to create a case study of a contemporary juvenile justice system on an Indian reservation in the Southwestern United States.

Davis, Laurence. (1959). Court reform in the Navajo Nation. <u>Journal of the American Judicature Society, 43</u> (2), 52-55.

Article traces the historical development of the tribal court system from its establishment in the Treaty of 1868. Author explores the evolution of tribal justice from its earlier primitive traditions to the current tribal court and appellate systems. Prior to 1959, jurisdiction over criminal and civil matters involving Indian defendants were shared between the federal government and the tribal council. Davis provides a detailed outline of the current tribal justice system and discusses jurisdictional challenges facing indigenous populations today.

Dean, S.B. (1968). <u>Law and order among the first Mississippians</u>.
National Institute of Law.

Text provides background information on law and American
Indians. Jurisdictional issues, including federal, tribal, and
major crimes are explored. Author focuses upon the health,
education, and economic factors involving Choctaw Indians
and how they affect crime rates. Text includes a proposed
Mississippi Choctaw code of laws.

Dumars, Charles T. (1968). Indictment under the 'Major Crimes Act':
An exercise in unfairness and unconstitutionality. <u>Arizona Law
Review, 10</u>, 691-705.

Article examines how the justice system treats Whites charged
with major crimes compared with how it treats Indians facing
the same charges. Research indicates that Indians receive
more severe penalties. Specifically, Indians are charged under
the Major Crimes Act, a federal statute with harsh sanctions.
Conversely Whites are charged under state laws, which have
less harsh penalties. The researcher concludes that all persons
committing the same crime, in the same geographical location,
should face the same treatment, regardless of race.

French, Laurence. (1981). Native American correctional treatment.
In Sloan Letman (Ed.), <u>Contemporary issues in corrections</u>
(pp.63-77). Cincinnati, OH: Pilgrimage Press.

Chapter examines the commonly-held perceptions of
American Indian culture and the tribal justice system. Specific
attention is directed to efforts being made by corrections
departments to rehabilitate Native American offenders.
Author outlines two approaches: the development of
correctional institutions exclusively for the handling of an
American Indian inmate population; and prison survival
schools for Native American offenders who are housed within
the general inmate populations. Chapter concludes with

discussion of Cheyenne Swift River Bird Project, an American Indian rehabilitation facility in Nebraska.

Grobsmith, Elizabeth S. (1989). The relationship between substance abuse and crime among Native American inmates in the Nebraska department of corrections. Human Organization, 48 (4), 285-298.

Study examines the impact of alcohol abuse on the rates of Native American incarceration. Research is based upon Nebraska prison records from 1986-1987 and ethnographic interviews. Interview data indicate a strong tie between early substance abuse and juvenile offending. Study also assesses the impact of Native American cultural and spiritual beliefs on offenders' rehabilitative efforts and suggestions for future research on American Indians.

Grobsmith, Elizabeth S. (1994). Indians in prison: Incarcerated Native Americans in Nebraska. Lincoln, NE: University of Nebraska Press.

Ethnographic study of American Indians incarcerated in Nebraska prisons. Text examines the increasing Native American population in prisons and its impact on Indian life. Comparing data on Native Americans incarcerated in other states, the author addresses reasons for the disproportionate representation of indigenous persons, relative to other groups.

Hagan, William T. (1966). Indian police and judges - Experiments in acculturation and control. New Haven, CT: Yale University Press.

Historical review of the development of a tribal police force in the 19th century. Author discusses creation of the agency as an alternative to the use of military troops and resources from the War Department. Hagan addresses how the merging of Native American customs with Anglo-Saxon jurisprudence resulted in a formal tribal justice system, but one which was far less formal than its White counterpart. Text focuses upon Sioux Indians.

Hermann, John Robert. (1995). American Indians in court: The Burger and Rehnquist years (1969-1992 terms) (Doctoral dissertation, Emory University, 1995). Dissertation Abstracts International, 56 (7), 2854.

Study explores the litigation efforts by American Indians within the context of a decision-making model of the United States Supreme Court. Author examines how interests of American Indians fared before the Court between 1969 and 1992. Data derived from U.S. Reports, U.S. Supreme Court Records and Briefs, Justices' private and public papers, and eleven interviews with staff attorneys at the Native American Rights Fund. Findings indicate that each Supreme Court Justice used different criteria to reach case decisions.

Kane, E. A. (1965). Jurisdiction over Indians and Indian reservations. Arizona Law Review, 6 (1), 237-255.

Article addresses the complexity surrounding the federal government's jurisdiction over Native Americans and their reservations. Author discusses instances where the jurisdiction of tribal courts, state governments, and federal laws may overlap and how such disputes are handled. Specifically, the issues surrounding crimes involving Indians and non-Indians are addressed.

Lujan, Carol C. (1995). Women warriors: American Indian women, crime, and alcohol. Women and Criminal Justice, 7 (1), 9-33.

Author examines issues of crime and alcohol among indigenous persons, with particular emphasis directed toward American Indian women. While young American Indian women are disproportionately represented in alcohol-related deaths in relation to the general female population, negative stereotypes have exaggerated both the rate of alcoholism and its association with crime among the American Indian population. Author argues factors contributing to misrepresentations include racist stereotyping, labeling, paternalism, language, and cultural differences. To counteract misinformation, author calls for additional research to be conducted through direct interaction with indigenous persons.

Meyer, J'ona F. (1998). History repeats itself: Restorative justice in Native American communities. Journal of Contemporary Criminal Justice, 14 (1), 42-57.

Article develops framework to explain the progression of Native American legal systems from one based upon restoration to one of retribution. Author notes tribal justice concepts began to change under the European colonization of indigenous cultures, which can be traced through five stages: aboriginal, tolerance, reduced tolerance, secrecy, and revitalization. Author presents a case study of the Navajo restorative justice system to illustrate this framework and discusses the future of restorative justice in Native American communities.

Minnis, Mhyra. (1963). The relationship of the social structure of an Indian community to adult and juvenile delinquency. Social Forces, 41 (4), 395-403.

Article focuses on the social structure of the Shashone-Bannock tribes and its impact on delinquency. Fieldwork, conducted in 1960, examines the tribes living conditions (e.g., type of housing, number of people in the household, and modernity). The sample of 189 families included 713 Indians. A five year review (1955-1960) of Indian arrest patterns indicates a gradual increase in delinquency. Most arrests, however, were for misdemeanor offenses (e.g., drunkenness). Author concludes that high delinquency rates are explained by a variety of factors including social, economic, community, and family structure.

Monikowski, Richard Arnold. (1997). The actual state of things: American Indians, Indian law and American courts between 1800 and 1835 (Doctoral dissertation, The University of New Mexico, 1997). Dissertation Abstracts International, 58 (1), 199.

"The actual state of things," was a phrase used by Chief Justice John Marshall in three of his most important opinions pertaining to the legal status of Indian people and tribes. Examining the historical development of Indian law, this study explores two controversial issues. First, Indian tribal use of non-Indian legal systems to determine their rights prior to 1831. Second, Indian law and tribal rights as espoused by Justice Marshall between 1801 and 1835, which differed significantly from Indian law as it was developed in state courts.

Nielsen, Marianne O., & Robert A. Silverman (Eds.). (1996). Native Americans, crime, and justice. Boulder, CO: Westview Press.

Inter-disciplinary anthology on Native American criminology. Includes essays by Native American and non-Native American scholars. Volume explores crime and justice issues, tribal versus federal jurisdiction on Indian lands, and the process of decision making in tribal courts. Contributors include: Ronet Bachman, Timothy Bynum, Ada Pecos Melton, Ray Paternoster, and Zoann Snyder-Joy.

Peak, Ken, & Jack Spencer. (1987). Crime in Indian country - Another 'Trail of Tears.' Journal of Criminal Justice, 15 (6), 485-494.

Article explores patterns of offending and arrest among

American Indians. Authors use trend analyses to examine total, adult, and juvenile arrests for total crimes, index offenses, as well as alcohol-related offenses. Comparisons with other racial and ethnic groups are explored, particularly for alcohol-related offenses. Frequency of crimes committed both on and off the reservation are also addressed.

Randall, Archie, & Bette Randall. (1978). Criminal justice and the American Indian. Indian Historian, 11 (2), 42-48.

Article attempts to explain the disproportionate arrest rate found in the American Indian population. Authors address the role negative stereotypes (e.g., the drunken Indian) play in the handling of Native American defendants in the criminal justice system (from arrest to sentencing). While these stereotypes do not solely explain their disproportionate arrest rates, the authors find that such expectations may lead to more arrests. Authors suggest such biases can be countered by increasing cultural awareness among criminal justice personnel and actively recruiting more Native American professionals to the justice system.

Reasons, Charles E. (1972). Crime and the Native American. In Charles Reason & Jack Kirkendall (Eds.), Race, crime and justice (pp.79-95).   Pacific Palisades, CA: Goodyear Publishing.

Article explores existing research on the disproportionate offending rates for Native Americans. Assessment of 1960s data which indicate that Native Americans had offending rates higher than all other racial groups. Author uses Uniform Crime Report data, from 1950-1969, to assess overall arrest rates and arrest patterns for specific offenses. These offending patterns are assessed in light of theoretical explanations, including economic, anomie, and cultural conflict. Author highlights impact of drinking on Native American offending rates.

Riffenburgh, Arthur S. (1964). Cultural influences and crime among
    Indian-Americans of the Southwest. Federal Probation, 28 (3),
    38-46.

    Article explores the "conduct-norms" of Indian-Americans.
    Specifically, author considers ways in which Indian-American
    culture conflicts with larger society. Research also looks at
    how these conduct norms impact group attitudes and behavior.
    The role of competition and the handling of money in some
    Indian cultures are among the topics discussed. Author
    considers how these cultural factors impact Indians who move
    from Indian communties to non-Indian cultures (e.g., urban
    areas). It is concluded that these differences impact how
    Indians are treated by the correctional system.

Ross, Luana. (1998). Inventing the savage: The social construction
    of Native American criminality. Austin, TX: University of
    Texas Press.

    Text explores historical and contemporary issues relating to
    Native American crime and criminality. Research includes
    interviews with incarcerated Native American women who
    discuss the impact of violence and criminal justice processing
    on their communities. Further, Ross evaluates the prevailing
    stereotypes of Native American culture, and how they impact
    upon proposed policies.

Samora, Julian, Joe Bernal, & Albert Pena. (1979). Gun powder
    justice: A reassessment of the Texas Rangers. Notre Dame,
    IN: University of Notre Dame Press.

    Text provides a detailed assessment of the Texas Rangers.
    Author considers the historical origins of the Rangers, impact
    of unchecked discretion on criminal enforcement, relationship
    to other Texas law enforcement officials, and ways in which
    they were used to control American Indian populations.

Shepardson, Mary. (1965). Problems of the Navajo tribal courts in transition. Human Organization, 24 (3), 250-53.

Article critiques efficacy of Navajo tribal courts. Author assesses whether tribal courts can become fully institutionalized. Provides historical overview and outline of Navajo courts and Navajo judges (since 1882). Discussion includes a comparison of the advantages of customary law with Navajo law. Author concludes that the use of the traditional Navajo legal system will decline as Indians increasingly adapt to Anglo-American culture.

Stanzell, Sharon. (1997). Assessment of law-violating youth and gangs: A psychosocial analysis of American Indian adolescents in Los Angeles County (Doctoral dissertation, California School of Professional Psychology - Los Angeles, 1997). Dissertation Abstracts International, 58 (9), 5142.

Based upon a sample of 83 American Indian adolescents ages 11 through 18, study examines the dynamics of delinquency through an examination of gang affiliation, law-violating youth groups, violence, and cultural identification. Specifically, author addressed whether factors, such as problem behaviors, psychological problems, parental drinking, exposure to domestic violence, or participation in traditional American Indian ceremonies affect gang membership. Findings indicate no differences between gang members and non-gang participants on most indicators, yet the former demonstrated higher levels of delinquent behavior, alcohol use, and drug use. Additionally, Apache youth were more likely to be involved in gangs and exhibit troubled behavior.

Stewart, Omer. (1964). Questions regarding American Indian criminality. Human Organization, 23, 61-66.

Article outlines the rates of Indian involvement in criminal offending, from 1957 to 1960. Several variables are analyzed including arrest rates, offense types, gender, and age. Intra-racial comparisons (e.g., different tribes) are included along with interracial comparisons (e.g., Indian, White, Negro). Author finds high rates of Indian criminality combined with high rates of alcohol abuse. It is concluded that these rates cannot be explained by race alone and much more study is necessary to explain high rates of Indian involvement in crime.

Taft, Philip B. (1981). Behind prison walls, Indians reclaim their heritage - A new political and cultural awareness combats the cycle of despair. Corrections Magazine, 7 (3), 6-15.

Article explores the role of social and economic factors in explaining crime among American Indians. Author notes the steady deterioration of traditional Native American customs in contemporary life, particularly among American Indian youth. Taft explores how this is being addressed within the criminal justice system, particularly through the offering of traditional activities (e.g., sweat lodges, pipe ceremonies, etc.) in some correctional facilities across the nation.

Wachtel, David. (1980). Historical look at BIA (Bureau of Indian Affairs) Police on the reservations. American Indian Journal, 6 (5), 13-18.

Article addresses jurisdictional issues involving the role of tribal police in handling non-Indian offenders on the reservation. Discussion of the landmark decision Oliphant v. Suquamish (1978), which negated the tribal courts inherent jurisdiction over non-Indian offenders, is included. Author notes that some have argued that this decision has negatively affected indigenous populations by opening up the reservation to non-Indian offenders and jurisdictional dilemmas. However, Wachtel suggests one possible solution may include the cross-jurisdictional deputization of tribal officers.

Williams, Larry E. (1976). Antecedents of urban Indian crime

(Doctoral dissertation, Brigham Young University, 1976). Dissertation Abstracts International, 37, 1832.

Dissertation examines scope of urban Indian crime, as well as degree of anti-Indian prejudice present in the judicial system. Author uses data obtained from questionnaires administered to American Indians and Whites and arrest records from a Seattle police department to explore causes of crime commited by Indians residing in urban centers. Analyses found prejudice surpassed both socio-economic and cultural indicators as a predictor of arrest.

Young, Thomas J. (1990). Native American crime and criminal justice require criminologists' attention. Journal of Criminal Justice Education, 1 (1), 111-116.

Author evaluates the representation of American Indians in twelve mainstream criminal justice textbooks. Analysis indicates that little attention is focused upon impact of crime on Native American communities. Author notes that studies show Native Americans suffer from one of the highest crime rates in the nation. Alcohol related arrest rates of Native Americans aged 14 and older are three times that of Blacks, and ten times that of Whites. Further, they have a higher arrest rate than any other racial or ethnic group in the U.S. These data, however, have had no noticeable impact on the representation of Native Americans in criminal justice texts. Author argues for a more inclusive and accurate portrayal of national crime patterns, specifically including Native Americans in future studies and criminology curriculum.

Zion, James W. (1998). Dynamics of Navajo peacemaking. Journal of Contemporary Criminal Justice, 14 (1), 58-74.

Article examines the revival and institutionalization of the traditional Navajo justice approach refered to as "peacemaking." This approach is the indigenous form of dispute resolution that is commonly referred to as "restorative justice" by criminologists. Author discusses the underlying goals associated with this model, as well as how it has been reintroduced into Navajo culture since 1982. Author found that the success of peacemaking was due to the change in attitude by parties, not the remedies this approach offers.

Part 3

Asian Americans

Alston, Jon P. (1976). Japanese and American attitudes toward the abolition of capital punishment. Criminology, 14 (2), 271-275.

Article compares national survey data on attitudes toward the abolition of the death penalty. Data collected in Japan and the United States. Analysis revealed that neither country favors a total ban, however, interpretation problems arose due to the disparate homicide rates between the two countries. Author addresses such differences, as well as cultural factors.

Bankston, Carl L., & Stephen J. Caldas. (1996). Adolescents and deviance in a Vietnamese-American community: A theoretical synthesis. Deviant Behavior, 17 (2), 159-181.

Ethnographic study based upon observations and interviews with people living in Vietnamese-American communities and resettlement camps. Authors explore reasons behind gang membership and delinquency among Vietnamese-American adolescents. An integrated theoretical model is offered to explain deviance patterns. This model draws from social integration, social learning, and labeling theories.

Bayley, David. (1976). Forces of order - Police behavior in Japan and the United States. Berkeley, CA: University of California

Press.

Ethnographic study provides detailed discussion on the
organization and activities of Japan's police force. Author
presents information in a comparative format to address
differences in activity and behavior between U.S. and Japanese
law enforcement agencies, as well as national crime rates.
Findings reveal significant differences in the two police
cultures, in addition to those found in the general social
structure. Bayley concludes that both factors contribute to the
lower crime rates observed in Japan.

Chin, Ko-Lin, Jeffrey Fagan, & Robert J. Kelly. (1992). Patterns
   of Chinese gang extortion. Justice Quarterly, 9 (4), 625-646.

Article explores patterns and social processes of gang
extortion. Based on 1990 survey data of 603 Chinese-owned
businesses in New York, authors evaluate how the political
economy and sociocultural contexts of the Chinese community
regulate and institutionalize gang victimization. Analyses
reveal that 69 percent of respondents had been approached by
Chinese gang members, and 54 percent had been victimized.
Authors conclude that the uniqueness of the political economy,
as well cultural norms and values within the Chinese
community, allow for the continuation of current levels of
gang extortion.

Dando, Shigemitsu. (1965). Japanese criminal procedure. South
   Hackensack, NJ: F.B. Rothman.

Text provides comprehensive overview of the Japanese legal
system for comparative purposes to the U.S. legal system.
Author begins with historical discussion of how Japanese law
developed and then outlines the basic structure of its courts
and adversarial system. Dando addresses some of the
commonalities between Japanese criminal procedures and U.S.
jurisprudence.

Hopkins, Julie A., Laurie A. Weinberg, & Mary Clement. (1994). Southeast Asian refugee youth: Implications for juvenile justice. Juvenile and Family Court Journal, 45 (2), 15-27.

Article examines Southeast Asian refugee youths. In recent years this group's delinquency rate has accelerated. Authors look at various socio-cultural factors which are unique to the life experiences of Southeast Asian juveniles. Particular attention is given to their problems of acculturation, the observed role reversal with parents, as well as the absence of parental guidance and mental health problems stemming from living in the war-torn environment of their home countries. The authors conclude that understanding these factors will enable the juvenile justice system to develop more effective delinquency prevention strategies.

Huston, Peter. (1995). Tongs, gangs, and triads: Chinese crime groups in North America. Boulder, CO: Paladin Press.

Text explores Chinese tradition of tongs, triads, and secret societies and their frequent involvement in organized crime, as well as their growing collusion with Chinatown street gangs. A historical overview of the social role of secret societies and the emergence and development of contemporary Chinatowns in North America is provided. The author explores those factors which are important to understanding Asian community responses to law enforcement and crime.

Jan, Lee. (1993). Asian gang problems and social policy solutions: A discussion and review. Gang Journal, 1 (4), 37-44.

Article examines the growing problem of Asian gangs in the United States and the origins of Asian organized crime groups. Author outlines how Asian gangs operate and the factors which contribute to their creation. Includes a discussion of intervention strategies developed to control Asian gang activities.

Joe, Karen A. (1994). The new criminal conspiracy? Asian gangs
and organized crime in San Francisco. Journal of Research in
Crime and Delinquency, 31 (4), 390-415.

Article based upon ethnographic interview data collected from
active and retired male members of Asian gangs in San
Francisco between 1990 and 1992. Author uses these data to
evaluate the relationship between gangs and organized crime
in view of current theoretical frameworks. Findings suggest
the links between Asian gangs and organized crime are best
conceptualized as associations between individuals and
groups, rather than criminal conspiracies. Author recommends
that future research focus on comparisons between Asian
gangs and other ethnic gangs, particularly on their similarities
and differences along cultural, familial, and immigration
experiences.

Johnson, Paula C. (1996). The social construction of identity in
criminal cases: Cinema verite and the pedagogy of *Vincent
Chin*. Michigan Journal of Race & Law, 1 (2), 348-489.

Article derives name from the 1989 documentary, "Who killed
Vincent Chin?" Johnson explores how both the doctrine and
application of law are informed by social constructions of
identity. Particularly, how race influences the administration
of justice in criminal cases. Divided into four parts, Johnson
first explores major theories of racial identity, with particular
attention directed toward the historical and contemporary
social construction of Asian American identity. Second,
events surrounding Vincent Chin's death are discussed to
provide contextual analysis of subsequent decisions made
during the criminal trial. Third, Johnson critiques the efficacy
of hate crime legislation. The final section concludes with the
argument that the effectiveness of hate crime laws ultimately
depends upon the rejection of social constructions that label
some racial groups as inferior to others.

Kitano, Harry H. L. (1967). Japanese-American crime and delinquency. Journal of Psychology, 66 (2), 253-263.

Article examines various explanations for low crime rates among Japanese American youth. Author surveyed 25 Japanese juvenile offenders and 37 Japanese non-delinquents. Findings revealed the delinquent sample differed from their non-delinquent counterparts on three factors: home life; ethnic relationships; and internalization of cultural norms. A significant proportion of the delinquent population came from broken homes, primarily socialized with non-Japanese peers, and were dissatisfied with their upbringing. Author concludes that an internalized sense of the traditional values inherent to the Japanese culture provides a strong form of social control.

Long, Patrick Du Phuoc, & Laura Ricard. (1997). The dream shattered: Vietnamese gangs in America. Boston: Northeastern University Press.

Drawing on ethnographic research with Vietnamese juvenile offenders in Santa Clara, California, text examines the nature of Vietnamese gang life, as well as explanations for gang involvement. The study indicates that many immigrant Vietnamese youth find it difficult to adapt to new surroundings, as well as American culture. This adjustment is further complicated by their new neighborhoods. These youth were more susceptible to involvement in gang activity and drug abuse. Authors conclude that current patterns will not change until there is a more developed analysis of Vietnamese youth acculturation.

Ma, Yue. (1993). Family relationships, broken homes, acculturation and delinquency in Chinese-American communities (Doctoral dissertation, Rutgers, the State University of New Jersey, 1993). Dissertation Abstracts International, 54 (3), 1102.

Study examines relationship between family and delinquency

in Chinese-American communities. Specifically, author looks at the effects that family and culture in Chinese-American communities have upon the likelihood of delinquency. Findings confirm that both family structure and relationships are significant predictors of delinquency. Chinese-American adolescents' beliefs in traditional Chinese values are inversely related to involvement in delinquency. Additionally, acculturation to American culture weakens childrens' beliefs in traditional cultural values, which further increases their likelihood of delinquency.

Pogrebin, Mark R., & Eric D. Poole. (1989). South Korean immigrants and crime: A case study. Journal of Ethnic Studies, 17 (3), 47-80.

Article explores the prevalence and causes of crime among Korean-Americans using data collected from a six-month field study with Korean immigrants. Authors focus on the role of imported cultural values in an explanation of crime among this population. Findings revealed a significant correlation between cultural factors and criminal activity, particularly in many Korean-American victims' unwillingness to cooperate with police. Authors recommend improvement in police-community relations between the Korean-American community and local law enforcement, with emphasis placed on increasing the reporting of crimes.

Poole, Eric D., & Mark R. Pogrebin. (1990). Crime and law enforcement policy in the Korean American community. Police Studies, 13 (2), 57-66.

Research based on field study of crime and law enforcement in the Korean community in Aurora, Colorado. Article evaluates reasons for the low rate of Asian American involvement, offending, and victimization in the criminal justice system. Authors explore cultural and structural explanations, such as group solidarity (based on high rate of recent immigrants) and reluctance to report crime to police. Findings indicate that government agencies should do more to integrate police-community services.

Rossman, Thomas A. (1978). Comparison study of the historical and sociological characteristics which have influenced the development and training of American and Oriental police systems (Doctoral dissertation, Wayne State University, 1978). Dissertation Abstracts International, 39 (3), 1868.

Dissertation compares sociological and structural characteristics between law enforcement agencies in China, Taiwan, Japan, and the United States. Author focuses on the influence cultural differences have on the attitudes and philosophy adopted by each agency. Study first compares the individual Oriental police agencies to one another, to the F.B.I. and to a local police department. Rossman argues differences can be attributed to the centralized nature of Oriental law enforcment agencies.

Sheu, Chuen-Jim. (1983). Assimilation, adaptation and juvenile delinquency among Chinese youths in New York Chinatown (Doctoral dissertation, State University of New York at Albany, 1983). Dissertation Abstracts International, 44 (6), 1934.

Dissertation examines factors contributing to delinquency among adolescent youth in New York's Chinatown. Data were derived from self-report surveys collected from 417 Chinese-American middle and high school aged students. Findings revealed that the greatest prevalence of delinquent behavior was among those youth who experienced alienation among their own native culture and had assimilated themselves into the American culture. Additionally, similar patterns of delinquency were found among both male and female Chinese-American adolescents.

Song, John Huey-Long. (1992). Attitudes of Chinese immigrants
      and Vietnamese refugees toward law enforcement in the
      United States. Justice Quarterly, 9 (4), 703-720.

      Study based on qualitative and quantitative survey data
      gathered from residents and community leaders in Chinese and
      Vietnamese communities in Orange and Los Angeles Counties.
      Research focuses on the interaction of recent Asian immigrants
      with American police and how concerns differ between the
      two groups. Analyses indicate that fear of crime, poor
      communication with police, and gang activities are the major
      concerns for Vietnamese respondents, while fear of crime and
      perceived police prejudice were the primary concerns for
      Chinese respondents. Vietnamese residents consistently rated
      these problems as more serious than their Chinese
      counterparts.

Song, John Huey-Long, John Dombrink, & Gilbert Geis. (1992).
      Lost in the melting pot: Asian youth gangs in the United
      States. Gang Journal, 1 (1), 1-12.

      Article examines the applicability of conventional
      criminological theories in understanding the structure and
      behavior of Chinese and Vietnamese youth gangs. Focus
      includes gang activity in San Francisco and New York.
      Authors conclude that while community disorganization may
      play a role in explaining the formation of Asian youth gangs,
      ability to cope with issues of identity and youth responses to
      law enforcement should also be included in causal models.

Wang, Zheng. (1995). Gang affiliation among Asian-American
      high school students: A path analysis of social developmental
      model 1. Journal of Gang Research, 2 (3), 1-13.

      Study uses a social developmental model to examine which
      factors influence gang affiliation among Asian American high
      school students. Data were derived from the 1992 National

Survey of Asian American High School Students. Analyses revealed causal relationships between gang affiliation and social bond, personality, cognitive skills, and social environmental factors. Author contends these relationships are best understood when a wide range of variables are examined.

Part 4

Hispanics

Bond-Maupin, Lisa, & James Maupin. (1998). Juvenile justice
    decision making in a rural Hispanic community. Journal of
    Criminal Justice, 26 (5), 373-384.

    Study examines processing of Hispanic youths through the
    juvenile justice system in two rural counties in New Mexico.
    Data were drawn from interviews with 591 Hispanic youths
    referred to the juvenile probation and parole office. Study
    found that these juveniles were subjected to considerable
    police surveillance and the communities' diversity affected the
    decision making of the juvenile justice professionals.

Carter, David L. (1983). Hispanic interaction with the criminal justice
    system in Texas: Experiences, attitudes and perceptions.
    Journal of Criminal Justice, 11 (3), 213-227.

    Exploratory study examines attitudes among Hispanics in
    Texas toward crime and the criminal justice system. Data
    were drawn from a mail sample of 312 Hispanic residents in
    Texas. Study found that Hispanics in Texas feel "less safe"
    from crime than the general population, that police cannot
    reduce crime, and evaluate the police less favorably than the
    general population. Hispanics feel that the criminal courts are
    generally fair and just and they also possess a strong punitive

attitude toward corrections.

Carter, David L. (1985). Hispanic perception of police performance:
An empirical assessment. Journal of Criminal Justice, 13 (6),
487-500.

Study evaluates Hispanics' perceptions of police performance
of random sample of 312 Hispanics in Texas. Respondents
were surveyed on their experience with and evaluations of
local police, sheriff officers, and the Texas Department of
Public Safety. Research indicates that any contact with police
lowered the rating of police performance. The fear of crime
and victimization among Hispanics also lowered evaluations
of local police. Respondents noted that police response time
and police investigation should be improved.

Diaz-Cotto, Juanita. (1996). Gender, ethnicity, and the state:
Latina and Latino prison politics. Albany, NY: State
University of New York.

Text focuses on prison politics in New York state and its
impact upon Latino prisoners. The Prisoners' Rights
Movement of the 1960s and 1970s and the Latino
community's response to the plight of Latino prisoners are
discussed. Text also explores the impact of post-Attica
reforms on Latinos imprisoned at Green Haven and Bedford
Hills correctional facilities (maximum security) in New York,
from 1970-1987. Includes a discussion of the conditions under
which Latino prisoners organized themselves to achieve
concessions from the state.

Farabee, David, Lynn Wallisch, & Jane Carlisle Maxwell. (1995).
Substance use among Texas Hispanics and non-Hispanics:
Who's using, who's not, and why. Hispanic Journal of
Behavioral Sciences, 17 (4), 523-536.

Article reports the findings of a telephone interview of 6,482

Hispanics and non-Hispanics. Respondents queried on the effects of acculturation on substance abuse. Specifically, study analyzes the inverse relationship between Hispanic culture and substance abuse among non-acculturated Hispanics, acculturated Hispanics, and non-Hispanics. Findings indicate that high-acculturated Hispanics report higher rates of alcohol and drug abuse than Mexican-born Hispanics (low-acculturated Hispanics). Additionally, Hispanics cite the importance of family and friends as a significant influence on their decision to abstain from alcohol and drug abuse, as compared to Whites who cite moral reasons.

Garcia, John. (1997). Latino national political survey, 1989-1990: Explorations into the political world of Mexican, Puerto Rican, and Cuban communities. Inter-University Consortium for Political and Social Research, 18 (1), 1-6.

Overview of the 1989 -1990 Latino National Political Survey which outlines Hispanic support for core American values, attitudes toward other groups in America, political attitudes toward social issues and policies, partisanship and electoral activities, political and organizational behaviors, and social networks and group identity. The study reports that Latinos favor increased governmental spending on crime, health, education, child services, and bilingual education. While survey results indicate that more Puerto Ricans and Mexicans are Democrats, and more Cubans are Republicans, party affiliations are diverse among Latinos.

Garcia, Robert. (1994). Latinos and criminal justice. Chicano-Latino Law Review, 14 (6), 6-29.

Article goes beyond the standard Black versus White discussion of crime and race. Discussion is focused on Latinos. Author uses the aftermath of the Rodney King/L.A.P.D. case to frame the analysis. Contrary to popular perception, the data show that 51 percent of the people arrested

were Latinos. In contrast, 38 percent were Black, 9 percent
White and 2 percent Asian Americans or Other. Further,
article considers theoretical explanations for Latino
involvement, victimization, and policy recommendations
based on findings.

Gertz, Marc, Laura Bedard, & Will Persons. (1995). Hispanic
perceptions of youth gangs: A descriptive exploration. Journal
of Gang Research, 2 (3), 37-49.

Article reveals the findings of a national opinion survey on
Hispanic attitudes on youth gangs. This diverse sample
showed dramatic disparity between what respondents believe
to be the cause of youth gang membership and what they
prescribe to prevent it. Approximately six percent of
respondents consider lack of jobs as the cause of gang
membership, while respondents overwhelmingly referenced
increased job opportunities as the best preventitive approach
to membership.

Harris, Mary G. (1988). Cholas: Latino girls and gangs. New York:
AMS Press.

Text offers a detailed consideration of Latino girl gangs.
Analysis is based upon a micro-structural assessment of girl
gang membership. Assessment is based upon interviews with
twenty-one girls, aged 13-21, conducted in 1981. The
participants were either involved in a gang at the time of the
study or had been at one time. The sample was drawn from
gangs which operate in the San Fernando Valley. These data
are compared and contrasted with interviews of criminal
justice professionals who interact with gangs (e.g., police
officers, probation officers), as well as family members.
Criminological theories (social disorganization, strain, and
control) are also evaluated. Study indicates that Latino girls
involved in gangs have weak familial and social ties and are
searching for a group identity.

LaFree, Gary D. (1985). Official reactions to Hispanic defendants in
the Southeast. Journal of Research in Crime and Delinquency,
22 (3), 213-237.

Study examines criminal justice outcomes for Hispanics by
comparing them to non-Hispanics. Data drawn from 755
defendants prosecuted during 1976-1977 for robbery or
burglary in El Paso, Texas, and Tucson, Arizona. Study found
that being Hispanic had no effect on the type of adjudication
received, verdict, or sentence severity in Tucson. In contrast,
El Paso Hispanics were more likely to be convicted in jury
trials and received more severe sentences. These differences
may be due to different mechanisms for providing attorneys
and different language difficulties.

Martinez, Ramiro F., Jr. (1996). Latinos and lethal violence: The
impact of poverty and inequality. Social Problems, 43 (2),
131-145.

Empirical analysis of the impact of poverty and economic
inequality on Latino homicide victims in 111 U.S. cities in
1980. Study examines the patterns and causes of Latino
homicide. Results show an inverse relationship between rates
of poverty and homicide. Findings also indicate that income
inequality is a leading predictor of Latino homicide.
Additionally, education attainment, city population, region,
and percentage of Latinos in city contribute to Latino crime
rate.

Martinez, Ramiro F., Jr. (1997). Homicide among the 1980 Mariel
refugees in Miami: Victims and offenders. Hispanic Journal
of Behavioral Sciences, 19 (2), 107-121.

Based upon data from the Miami Police Department, Homicide
Investigations Unit, study examines homicide and offense and
victimization patterns for Mariel, Cuban immigrants.
Comparative analysis of Mariel Cubans with Cubans who

immigrated to the U.S. prior to 1980. Article provides a theoretical and empirical overview of research on immigration and crime. Research findings indicate that Mariels have a higher homicide rate than their rate in the population. Further, Mariels were found to face a greater risk of harm than other Cubans in Miami. Author concludes that more research on homicide among Latinos is necessary (e.g., Central Americans and Mexicans), particularly given their growing numbers in the U.S.

Martinez, Ramiro F., Jr. (1999). Latinos and homicide. In M. Dwayne Smith & Margaret Zahn (Eds.), Studying and preventing homicide (pp.143-158). Thousand Oaks, CA: Sage.

Martinez notes that most of the research on homicide rates and race is on Whites and Blacks. He argues that Latinos are largely and inexplicably overlooked in these discussions. The size of the Latino population, as well as the impact of homicide on Latino communities, make it necessary to include them in analyses of race and lethal violence. Article evaluates how Latinos are categorized by race for official data, provides an overview of historical and contemporary studies of Latino homicide, and considers the suggested link between immigration and homicide rates.

Mirande, Alfred. (1987). Gringo justice. Notre Dame, IN: University of Notre Dame Press.

Text offers one of the few detailed assessments of Chicanos and the criminal justice system. Discussion underscores and assesses the discriminatory treatment Chicanos have faced since the end of the war between Mexico and the U.S. Author addresses a wide range of issues, including immigration, Chicano stereotypes, border patrol, and police-Chicano community relations. Mirande argues for developing a theory of "Gringo Justice," which would include the perspectives of Chicanos in social science and sociology.

Rodriguez, Michel, & Claire Brindis. (1995). Violence and Latino youth: Prevention and methodological issues. Public Health Reports, 110 (3), 260-267.

Article explores the relationship between culture and violence for Latino youths. Authors present an overview of the scope of homicide and intentional injuries in Latino communities, review risk factors for intentional injuries, and discuss the implications of ethnic-specific factors for violence prevention and research efforts. Data collection and methodological issues, and their implications for violence prevention research are addressed.

Simpson, D. Dwayne, & Michel Barrett. (1991). A longitudinal study of inhalant use: Overview and discussion of findings. Hispanic Journal of Behavioral Sciences, 13 (2), 341-355.

Article reports findings of a four-year longitudinal study of inhalant use among 100 Mexican-American youths admitted to the Youth Advocacy Program in Austin, Texas, between 1981 and 1985. Study found that juveniles use inhalants for various reasons, including: availability, curiosity, and the sensation produced. Report also assesses youths' medical and psychological health, as well as family and peer relations. Further, impact of socio-economic disadvantages, discrimination, and acculturation are discussed.

Sommers, Ira, Jeffrey Fagan, & Deborah Baskin. (1993). Sociocultural influences on the explanation of delinquency for Puerto Rican youths. Hispanic Journal of Behavioral Sciences, 15 (1), 36-62.

Examination of self-reported drug use and delinquency among Puerto Rican male adolescents in the South Bronx. In the first wave of this longitudinal survey researchers employed a multi-stage, cluster sampling design to study 1,077 Puerto Rican males, ages 12 and 19 years old. Findings indicate that acculturation is positively associated with participation in interpersonal violence and theft. Lower acculturation, however, is related to participation in illicit drug use.

Ven, Thomas Vander. (1998). Fear of victimization and the interactional construction of harassment in a Latino neighborhood. Journal of Contemporary Ethnography, 27 (3), 374-398.

Ten-month ethnographic study on fear of victimization reported by residents in a predominantly Latino neighborhood in Washington, D.C. Author hypothesized that when one pedestrian fears another, the apprehensive pedestrian sometimes communicates feelings of vulnerability by using overt avoidance techniques or by acting cautious. The feared individual may respond by acting in a threatening or dangerous manner. Author found that outsiders who walked into the community with a preconceived notion of the local men as potential predators were often unwilling partners in their own harassment. It is concluded that fearful behavior acts as temporary labeling, which serves as an invitation to harass a clearly vulnerable individual. This labeling may have long-term consequences if men are consistently perceived as dangerous.

Part 5

African Americans

Bell, Derrick. (1992). Race, racism and American law. Boston: Little, Brown and Company.

Text covers a broad spectrum of issues relating to anti-Black racism and U.S. legal institutions. Specifically, author explores slavery, miscegenation laws, and segregation in public facilities. Focus is on ways in which Black citizenship has been suppressed. Specifically, a consideration of the denial of voting rights and discrimination in the administration of justice. Additionally, Bell outlines how the law has been used in the battle for effective public schools, fair housing, and fair employment.

Berlin, Ira, Marc Favreau, & Steven F. Miller (Eds.). (1998). Remembering slavery: African Americans talk about their personal experiences of slavery and emancipation. New York: New Press.

Based upon 1930s research conducted by the Works Progress Administration [W.P.A.]. Includes narrative text of interviews with nine Black former slaves, who discuss a variety of topics. These former slaves describe in detail the inhumane conditions of slavery. They tell stories of the back-breaking field labor, difficulty of keeping families together, their relationships with other slaves, slaveholders, slave culture, and the impact of the Civil War.

Bernard, Thomas J. (1990). Angry aggression among the "truly disadvantaged." Criminology, 28 (1), 73-96.

Article challenges existing subcultural theories as incomplete in explaining violence arising from trivial incidents. Bernard explores individual and aggregate-level explanations for homicides involving unrelated, lower-class males, who are disproportionately Black. Analysis focuses on psychological and biological research findings that "cognitive rules" are essential to understanding anger and aggression. Additionally, Bernard incorporates William J. Wilson's argument on the "truly disadvantaged" into his analysis. Article concludes that a structural theory of angry aggression is indicated.

Blake, Wayne M., & Carol A. Darling. (1994). The dilemmas of the African American male. Journal of Black Studies, 24 (4), 402-415.

Article examines the reasons for the "disappearing African American male." Discussion of how substance abuse, suicide, education, economics, employment issues, violence, discrimination, and family relations impact this phenomenon. Authors conclude that shorter life expectancy and high mortality rates explain declines in the Black male population. Further, authors encourage a multi-institutional approach (e.g., education, employment) to evaluate Black male involvement in the criminal justice system.

Brown, William B. (1998). The fight for survival: African-American gang members and their families in a segregated society. Juvenile and Family Court Journal, 49 (2), 1-14.

Study examines structural and racial barriers faced by gang members and their parents. Based upon qualitative and quantitative data collected from 74 Detroit gang members and 68 of their parents or guardians (1992-1996), author explores effects of racial discrimination and segregation on gang involvement. Although many of the parents attempted to dissuade their children from involvement in gangs, findings revealed affiliation was interpreted by the youth as not so much a choice, but as necessary for survival.

Bruce, Marino A., Vincent J. Roscigno, & Patricia L. McCall. (1998). Structure, context, and agency in the reproduction of Black-on-Black violence. Theoretical Criminology, 2 (1), 29-55.

Article presents an overview and critique of mainstream theories offered to explain violence by Blacks. Authors review micro-level and macro-level explanations of offending and find both inadequate. For example, authors reject the subculture of violence thesis and other sub-cultural approaches as skewed. They conclude that dynamic theoretical models are required, ones which take into account both normative and structural processes.

Burns, Haywood. (1972). Can a Black man get a fair trial in this country? In George F. Cole (Ed.), Criminal justice: Law and politics (pp. 391-418). North Scituate, MA: Duxbury Press.

Exploration of how the historical treatment of Blacks affects their experience in the criminal justice system. Essay offers numerous examples to establish that the current system is infected with holdovers of past racism. Examples offered include ways in which judges refer to Blacks in court, harsher sanctions faced by Black offenders, and longer time served by Black inmates. Author concludes that Blacks will receive equitable treatment within the criminal justice system once they receive it in larger society.

Butler, Paul. (1996). Racially based jury nullification: Black

power in the criminal justice system. Yale Law Journal, 105
(3), 677-725.

Essay examines practice of jury nullification by African
American jurors. Author argues its legitimacy, asserting that
for some nonviolent offenders, the Black community reaps a
greater benefit if offenders are allowed to remain in the
community, rather than placed in a correctional institution.
Butler's argument is based on the exponential increase in
Black incarceration rates. Decisions as to which offenders
should be sanctioned should rest with community members,
rather than the criminal justice system.

Butler, Paul. (1997). Affirmative action and the criminal law.
University of Colorado Law Review, 68 (4), 841-889.

Author observes that Blacks are overrepresented in most
indicators of social dysfunction, including arrest, incarceration,
low education, and unemployment. At the same time, Blacks
are underrepresented in most indicators of social success.
Butler takes the position that affirmative action, which has
been used to equal the balance in voting, education, and
employment, is likewise applicable in the criminal justice
system. Well-developed arguments are followed by six
proposals for "affirmative action for Black criminal
defendants."

Caldwell, Loretta, & Helen E. Taylor Greene. (1980). Implementing
a Black perspective in criminal justice. In Alvin W. Cohn &
Benjamin Ward (Eds.), Improving management in criminal
justice (pp. 143-156). Thousand Oaks, CA: Sage.

Chapter addresses the underrepresentation of Blacks as
policymakers, criminal justice personnel, and criminologists.
The exclusion of African Americans from these positions has
resulted in the absence of a Black perspective on crime, as well
as the development of effective crime control strategies.

Authors recommend increased efforts to recruit Black professionals within the criminal justice system, as well as at the nation's univeristies.

Cao, Liqun, Adams A. Jensen, & Vickie J. Jensen. (1997). A test of the Black subculture of violence thesis: A research note. Criminology, 35 (2), 367-379.

Test of the subculture of violence thesis. Data from the General Social Survey, 1983-1991. Analysis includes data for 3,218 people, 12 percent were African-American. Three measures, which combined "violent defensive" and "violent offensive" values, were used for the dependent variable (subculture of violence). Independent variables include race, age, education, income, region and employment. Findings indicate that White males are significantly more likely than Blacks to express violent tendencies in defensive circumstances. Authors, therefore, reject the subcultural theory which posits that a unique culture of violence permeates the Black population.

Chideya, Farai. (1995). Don't believe the hype: Fighting cultural misinformation about African Americans. New York: Penguin.

Text aims to dispel the negative stereotypes and misinformation perpetuated about African Americans. Chideya provides an array of facts and figures on Blacks in the U.S. Text includes "Racial Issues I.Q. Quiz" and comparative data for Blacks and Whites on employment, education, welfare, crime, politics, and affirmative action.

Clarke, James W. (1996). Black-on-Black violence. Society, 33 (5), 46-50.

Author analyzes the roots of Black-on-Black violence in the U.S. Clarke concludes that current trends are rooted in the nineteenth century's Southern criminal justice system model, which granted immunity for crimes committed against Blacks and condoned Black-on-Black violence.

Collins, Catherine Fisher. (1997). The imprisonment of African American women: Causes, conditions, and future implications. Jefferson, NC: McFarland.

Text provides a historical analysis of Black women in the criminal justice system. Current imprisonment trends for Black females are also discussed. Author argues current patterns are the result of the criminal justice system's inability to address the needs of this population and the failure of government in addressing the underlying causes of crime.

Covington, Jeanette. (1995). Racial classification in criminology: The reproduction of racialized crime. Sociological Forum, 10 (4), 547-568.

Article explores how criminologists and their research methods are affected by society-wide beliefs about crime and race. Author evaluates how hypotheses are formulated and inform racial comparisons used to explain crime. These explanations, largely based on phenotype, are used to justify control of minorities not involved in crime.

Crawford, Charles, Ted Chiricos, & Gary Kleck. (1998). Race, racial threat and sentencing of habitual offenders. Criminology, 36 (3), 481-511.

Study empirically assesses how habitual offender statutes impact the decision to prosecute. Analysis is based upon data for approximately 10,000 male repeat offenders admitted to Florida prisons between 1992-1993. Logistic regression, which controlled for crime seriousness and prior record, showed significant race effect. Race effect was particularly pronounced for Black offenders charged with drug-related offenses, larceny, and burglary. Empirical findings are used to evaluate "racial threat" theory of sentencing outcomes.

Curtis, Lynn A. (1975). Violence, race and culture. Lexington, KY: Lexington Books.

Text explores cultural interpretations of Black violence, focusing on homicide, rape, robbery, and aggravated assault. Specifically, Curtis addresses the various theories offered to explain Black offending, including anomie and subculture-of-violence. Author evaluates existing theories with the goal of interpreting the impact of culture on crime and recommending directions for future research and policy considerations.

Davis, Angela. (1997). Race and criminalization. In Wahneema Lubiano (Ed.), The house that race built (pp.264-279). New York: Pantheon.

Detailed discussion and overview of the problems associated with rising rates of incarceration in the U.S. Davis focuses on the impact on these increased rates on Blacks and the increasing number of privately-owned prisons. Analysis of how current trends mirror historical treatment of Blacks. Davis notes that mainstream analysis frequently overlook how these rising rates impact women. Specifically, that the incarceration rates for women, notably women of color, are rising more rapidly than for men. Davis concludes that prisons should be abolished.

DiIulio, John J. (1994). The question of Black crime. The Public Interest, 117, 3-32.

Essay argues that the nation's crime problem is, in essence, an inner-city problem. Author draws upon official data to demonstrate the increasing gap between Black and White rates of victimization and perpetration of violent crimes. To halt this pattern, the author proposes four crime control measures:

remedial measures to secure inner-city neighborhoods; increased police presence; increased rate of incarceration for both violent and repeat offenders; and removal of severely neglected and abused children from inner-city homes. Includes commentary by Patrick Langan, Glenn Loury, Paul Robinson, and James Q. Wilson.

Dorsey, L.C. (1994). Black women in prison: Redefining a women's place. In Vasilikie Demos, & Marcia Texler Segal (Eds.), Ethnic women: A multiple status reality (pp.261-273). Dix Hills, NY: General Hall.

Chapter uses national statistics to examine the status of Black women in the U.S. criminal justice system. Since the 1970s, arrests of women have increased at a rate faster than men. It is noted that Black women are disproportionately represented in the prison population. High rates of female poverty explain their high rates of economic crimes. Poverty, when combined with racism and sexism, place Black women in triple jeopardy of becoming involved in the system.

Dulaney, Marvin. (1996). Black police in America. Bloomington, IN: Indiana University Press.

Historical overview of Blacks in law enforcement, covering post-Civil War period through the 1980s. Text provides a comprehensive study of the origin, role, accomplishments, and experiences of Black police officers throughout the U.S. Topic areas include: nexus between slavery and the development of the first formal law enforcement agencies; effects of the political patronage in the North on the integration of Blacks into policing; rise of Black officers to administrative and leadership positions; and overall look at treatment and experiences of Black officers within and outside police departments.

Durrant, Robert H., Robert A. Pendergrast, & Chris Cadenhead.

(1994). Exposure to violence and victimization and fighting behavior by urban Black adolescents. Journal of Adolescent Health, 15 (4), 311-318.

Data from a cross-sectional survey of 225 Black youths, ages 11-19, living in or around nine Housing and Urban Development projects. Two hypotheses are tested. First, whether exposure to violence and personal victimization are associated with the frequency with which adolescents engage in fighting behaviors; and second, whether adolescents who are goal-oriented and from more secure families report less fighting behavior. Analyses provide support for both hypotheses.

Farrell, Walter C., Jr., James H. Johnson, Jr., Marty Sapp, Roger M. Pumphrey, & Shirley Freeman. (1995). Redirecting the lives of urban Black males: An assessment of Milwaukee's Midnight Basketball League. Journal of Community Practice, 2 (4), 91-107.

Survey data from 96 participants in Milwaukee's Midnight Basketball League. Results indicate that the returns on money invested in the program are far greater than those from more traditional punitive programs and policies. The program was found to aid in the reduction of crime, provide a safe and stable environment for youth, and serve as a nexus for improved educational and career aspirations for program participants.

Felkenes, George T., & Jean Reith Schroedel. (1993). A case study of minority women in policing. Women and Criminal Justice, 4 (2), 65-89.

Drawing from cross-sectional survey of 1,041 Black female officers in the Los Angeles Police Department, departmental records and the findings of the Christopher Commission. Article explores the experiences of minority women in policing. While analysis revealed that minority females constitute a larger proportion of total female officers than hypothesized, they were still underrepresented within policing. Authors conclude that the observed pattern may be the result of high attrition and recycling rates in the police academy. Further, the disproportionately low rate of female officers may reflect dissatisfaction with their training.

Free, Marvin D., Jr. (1996). African Americans and the criminal justice system. New York: Garland.

Text provides a comprehensive overview of African Americans and the criminal justice system. Specifically, author addresses the Black experience in America, theoretical explanations of African American involvement in crime, and African American treatment by the police, courts and corrections. Free also looks at the role of Black professionals within the justice system. He concludes that improved economic conditions will reduce crime and that more Black criminal justice professionals, such as professors and judges are needed.

Free, Marvin D., Jr. (1999). Racial issues in contemporary criminology textbooks: The case of African-Americans. Contemporary Justice Review, 1 (4), 429-466.

Comprehensive analysis of race in 18 criminology textbooks, published between 1994-1997. Research focuses on two broad issues. First, whether the work of African-American criminologists are incorporated. Second, whether and how issues pertaining to African-Americans are presented. Free's study utilizes five measures to evaluate texts: how race is conceptualized; how African-Americans are portrayed in text language and photographs; how Black crime is discussed; degree to which African-American perspectives are incorporated; and how issues of special import to the Black community are presented. Findings indicate that textbooks do not adequately present a historical perspective on race, little attention is focused on the scholarship of African-American criminologists, cursory attention is given to the social construction of race, and issues relating to Black communities are inadequately covered.

Freeman, Richard B. (1987). The relation of criminal activity to Black youth employment. The Review of Black Political Economy, 16, 98-107.

Evaluation of the impact of criminal activity on employment rates for Black males in high poverty neighborhoods. Specific focus on out-of-work Black males, aged 16-24. Research based on 1979-1980 National Bureau of Economic Research. Included 2,400 inner-city youths who provided self-report data on activities, employment, education, church attendance, residence, grades, household size, and drug use. Findings indicate that involvement in crime substantially reduces likelihood of employment.

French, Laurence. (1983). Profile of the incarcerated Black female offender. Prison Journal, 63 (2), 80-87.

Literature review of research examining the characteristics of incarcerated Black female offenders in both adult and juvenile facilities. Similar patterns were found between the juvenile and adult samples. In both institutions, Black females were found to adopt a leadership position and hold a higher social status among the general inmate population. Additionally, research consistently indicates that Black females are overrepresented at all stages of the criminal justice process and receive harsher treatment than their non-Black counterparts.

Gabbidon, Shaun L. (1996). An argument for including W.E.B. Du Bois in the criminology/criminal justice literature. Journal of Criminal Justice Education, 7 (1), 99-112.

A review of W.E.B. Du Bois' pioneering work on crime and

race. Author argues that this extensive scholarship should be part of the criminology curriculum. Article provides insight into the breadth of Du Bois' writings, analysis of why his work has been overlooked, various theoretical classifications for his work, and his impact upon the discipline of criminology.

Gray-Ray, Phyllis, Melvin C. Ray, Sandra Rutland, & Sharon Turner. (1995). African Americans and the criminal justice system. Humboldt Journal of Social Relations, 21 (2), 105-117.

General overview of research on impact of race in the justice system. Article looks at victimization rates for Blacks compared with other racial groups, arrest rates for index offenses by race, and sentencing and corrections data. Though the article focuses on the experience Black adults have with the justice system, the impressions of Black youths are considered as well.

Greene, Helen. (1981). Black women in the criminal justice system. Urban League Review, 6 (1), 55-61.

Article provides an overview of the existing data on Black women in the criminal justice system. Author notes that though there is more information available today on Black females than in the past, there is still a large amount of missing data. Article reviews treatment of Black women at various stages of the justice process: arrest, booking, pre-trial confinement, sentencing, and incarceration. It is concluded that Black females face unique challenges within the criminal justice system due to their class status. Further, more data are needed on the impact of prison on child-rearing, participation rates of Black women in alternative programs, and an overall needs assessment of Black females in the justice system.

Gunst, Laurie. (1995). Born fi' dead: A journey through the Jamaican posse underworld. New York: Henry Holt.

Based on ten years of field data, the author provides an overview of Jamaican posses. Tracing the inception of this subculture from Kingston, Gunst explores the mercenary role members initially served as street fighters for local politicians. In the early 1980s, Jamaican posses migrated to the United States, where they gained a reputation for violence in the crack cocaine market. Author observes that criminological research on these posses is limited since few survive the violence of the drug trade.

Hadjor, Kofi Buenor. (1997). Race, riots and clouds of ideological smoke. Race and Class, 38 (4), 15-31.

A review of how urban unrest and riots have been analyzed by the popular press and academic research. Hadjor uses the unrest which followed the Rodney King/L.A.P.D. acquittal to analyze how such incidents are reported. He finds that Black inner-city residents are typically blamed for outbreaks, regardless of facts. Further, he notes that the mainstream press frequently attempts to make distinctions between the precipitating conditions and the unrest itself. Hadjor considers various ideological analyses of urban unrest, such as "riff-raff" theories of rioting.

Hawkins, Darnell F. (1990). Explaining the Black homicide rate. Journal of Interpersonal Violence, 5 (2), 151-163.

Explanations for the high rate of homicide among Blacks, in comparison to other racial groups, are summarized and critiqued. Author contends that contemporary research has erroneously focused on quantitative rather than theoretical assessments in its explanation of observed rate differences. Specifically, disproportionate offending is often explained by internal factors, such as a subculture of violence or genetic predisposition theories. Author concludes that research which seeks to explain differences in crime rates by race must be re-directed to include external factors, such as social and economic inequality.

Hawkins, Darnell F. (1999). African Americans and homicide. In
M. Dwayne Smith, & Margaret Zahn (Eds.), Studying and
preventing homicide (pp.143-158). Thousand Oaks, CA: Sage.

Highlights and discusses the shortcomings of existing research
on homicide. Specific focus on the impact that ethnicity and
class have on homicide rates. Hawkins argues that research on
homicide should be disaggregated by race. This would allow
for a more nuanced analysis of the relationship between race,
ethnicity, and crime and allow for the study of sub-populations
within various racial groups. Hawkins compares and analyzes
Black and White homicide rates as an example of "thoughtful
disaggregation."

Heard, Chinita, W. G. Ludwig, & Robert Bing. (1996). Correlates
of drug use among African American arrestees: The case for
multicultural approaches. The Journal of Research on
Minority Affairs, 3 (1), 3-10.

Researchers examine the need for treatment-based strategies
with multicultural services and sensitivity training. Analysis
focuses upon demographic characteristics of arrestees who
tested positive for drug use while in custody at a Fort Wayne,
Indiana correctional facility. Findings indicate that Whites
were most likely to need drug treatment for alcohol, while
Blacks were most likely to need drug treatment for crack
cocaine.

Higginbotham, A. Leon, Jr. (1996). Shades of freedom: Racial
politics and presumptions of the American legal process. New
York: Oxford University Press.

Text offers a historical critique of the U.S. criminal justice
system. Author analyzes 19th and 20th century legal decision-
making on race (e.g., 1883 Civil Rights cases and Plessy v.

Ferguson) and its evolution and impact on criminal justice processing today. Text concludes with "ten precepts of American slavery jurisprudence." This volume is Higginbotham's second book in a series on Race and the American Legal Process. In the Matter of Color (1978) was the first book.

Jackson, Pamela Irving. (1992). Minority group threat, social context, and policing. In Allen E. Liska (Ed.), Social threat and social control (pp.89-101). Albany, NY: State University of New York Press.

An evaluation of the empirical literature on policing in minority communities. Specifically, Jackson considers the historical and contemporary impact of minority group threat on police responses to crime by Blacks who live and work in close proximity to Whites. Enforcement of anti-gang and drug laws are discussed. Chapter analyzes social context of minority group threat, such as city size, region, and proximity.

Jenkins, Philip. (1993). African-Americans and serial homicide. American Journal of Criminal Justice, 17 (2), 47-60.

Using data drawn from 1971 to 1990, study investigates the involvement of African-Americans in serial homicides. Author found 13 of the 100 cases examined involved Black offenders, yet a "White" image is typically associated with serial murderers. It is concluded that this media and law enforcement stereotype may lead to the neglect of minority victims and their communities.

Johnson, Paula C. (1995). At the intersection of injustice: Experiences of African American women in crime and sentencing. American University Journal of Gender & the Law, 4 (1), 1-76.

Detailed critique of how African American women are processed through the U.S. criminal justice system. Johnson argues that the standard race versus gender discussions of crime have meant that African American women are largely overlooked in analyses of the justice system. Article highlights the case of Angela Thompson, a young Black woman convicted of selling crack cocaine and sentenced to a mandatory minimum sentence of fifteen years. Johnson notes the rising population of women offenders who are increasingly convicted of drug-related crimes. Additionally, article provides both a historical and contemporary overview of the treatment of African American women by the justice system.

Johnson, Sheri Lynn. (1993). Racial imagery in criminal cases. Tulane Law Review, 67 (6), 1739-1805.

Article assesses the degree to which racial imagery, particularly Blackness, affects outcomes in criminal cases. Johnson provides detailed review of how racial imagery is used during various phases of a trial, including pretrial publicity, witness testimony, and closing arguments. Argument is based largely on case anecdotes. Johnson uses testimony in the Rodney King/L.A.P.D. criminal case to show how race imagery was employed to signal deep-seated fears of Black men (e.g., testimony that King gave a "bear like yell"). Johnson concludes that "race shield laws" should be adopted to ensure that racial imagery is not exploited and does not lead to unjust results.

Jones, Clinton B. (1979). The criminal justice/racial justice nexus. In R.G. Iacovetta, & Dae H. Chang (Eds.), Critical issues in criminal justice (pp. 22-36).

Essay considers the link between racial issues and criminal justice issues. Paper outlines the shifting forms of racial discrimination, beginning with slavery and Jim Crow. While the earlier forms represent intentional race discrimination, the contemporary forms (1954-1976) represent institutional racism. This latter type (e.g., racial discrimination practiced by criminal justice system professionals), though subtle, is at least as formidable as earlier manifestations. Chapter reviews programs and policies that were designed to enhance Black support for the criminal justice system.

Jones, Terry. (1978). Blacks in the American criminal justice system: A study of sanctioned deviance. Journal of Sociology and Social Welfare, 5 (3), 356-373.

Article considers ways in which Black professionals can improve racial conditions within the criminal justice system. Author reviews the numerical representation of Blacks within the justice system as judges, correctional officers, and social workers. Jones explores variety of issues, including whether Blacks who are employed by the system are part of the problem and whether they can realistically affect change.

Joseph, Janice. (1995). Black youths, delinquency, and juvenile justice. Westport, CT: Praeger.

Text examines some of the key issues surrounding the relationship between being an African American youth and involvement in the nation's juvenile justice system. Author argues that traditional theories of delinquency are inadequate at explaining Black delinquency. Specifically, these theories do not adequately address socio-historical influences. Author argues that the traditional response of increased sanctions will not solve the problem of youth violence. Prevention efforts, therefore, should focus on earlier, long-term interventions.

King, Anthony E.O. (1993). African-American males in prison: Are they doing time or is time doing them? Journal of Sociology & Social Welfare, 20 (1), 9-27.

King explores the impact of incarceration on Black men. Article focuses on the need to evaluate the prison experience, such as violence and drug abuse, and the affects of these on social and psychological well-being. King also discusses how the incarceration problem affects not only those who are in prison, and their bonds with family members, but also the impact on the communities they come from. Author concludes that study in this area is particularly important given that Black men comprise a disproportionate share of the incarcerated population.

Laub, John, & Joan McDermott. (1985). An analysis of serious crime by young Black women. Criminology, 23 (1), 81-98.

Study examines a virtually untouched area of research and empirical focus, Black female juvenile offending. Article provides an overview of existing theories and research on Black female offending. Authors use National Crime Survey data, (1973-1981), to evaluate and compare the offending patterns of Black females, Black males, White females, and White males. Findings indicate a link between female/male offending patterns across race, when crime seriousness is taken into account. Further, data indicate a convergence between Black female offending and White female offending patterns. Authors encourage additional research on Black female criminality.

Lemelle, Anthony J., Jr. (1995). Black male deviance. Westport, CT: Praeger.

Text provides detailed discussion of sociological and theoretical treatments of race, including a critique of race and theories of deviance (e.g., anomie and internal colonialism). Lemelle analyzes how Black men experience race and how they are viewed by other races and how this in turn affects behavior. Discussion includes historical overview, political analysis of race, and intersections of class, race, and gender.

Letcher, Maxine. (1979). Black women and homicide. In Harold M. Rose (Ed.), Lethal aspects of urban violence (pp. 83-90).

Lexington, MA: Lexington Books.

Chapter focuses on lethal violence by Black women. Author notes that this issue has received little academic attention. This is partly explained by low levels of female offending. Chapter evaluates how to bridge this gap in research. Specifically, author outlines subcultural theories which have been used to explain female offending. Next, there is a consideration of the social science stereotypes of Black women and how these may impact research. Author concludes that more research should be devoted to developing a model which explains Black female offending.

Lewis, Diane K. (1981). Black women offenders and criminal justice: Some theoretical considerations. In Marguerite A. Warren (Ed.), Comparing female and male offenders (pp. 89-105). Beverly Hills, CA: Sage.

Research tackles disproportionate crime rates of Black women offenders. Author notes that Black women have fallen through the cracks of research on crime. The existing research on female offending is limited to White women and the available research on race is focused on Black men. Article provides a statistical overview of Black female offending and outlines the existing models of Black female criminality (e.g., economic deprivation, racism, status equality, socialization, sexism). This assessment indicates that current theoretical models are fragmented, speculative and incomplete. Well-developed theories are needed to deepen our understanding of crime by Black women.

Love, R. B. (1980). Educational process and Black on Black crime. Arlington, VA: Eric Document Reproduction Service.

Research addresses the nature of Black on Black crime, particularly among African American youth. Author argues this phenomenon is a reflection of institutional racism and

economic deprivation within inner-city communities. To
combat the problem, a more positive environment needs to be
established -- through in-school educational programs (e.g.,
conflict resolution training, tutoring, etc.) and mentoring
organizations.

Maclin, Tracey. (1998). Race and the Fourth Amendment.
   Vanderbilt Law Review, 51 (2), 333-393.

Comprehensive overview of how search and seizure laws have
been used to control Black populations. Maclin begins with a
historical analysis of how police monitored Black movement
and how this past is reflected in today's police practices. This
background informs Maclin's thesis that the police are more
likely to subject Black and Hispanic motorists to arbitrary
stops. This analysis is buttressed with a critique of U.S.
Supreme Court decisions, including, *Whren v. U.S.* (1996).
Maclin concludes that where a minority motorist has been
arrested following a routine traffic stop, prosecutors should be
required to provide a race-neutral explanation beyond a traffic
infraction.

Mauer, Marc. (1999). Race to incarcerate. New York: The New York
   Press.

An evaluation of the increasing rate of Black imprisonment in
the U.S. Mauer examines the relationship between criminal
justice reality and policy prescriptions; media representations
of crime; and the politicization of criminal justice issues. Text
provides a detailed analysis of the increasing rate of
incarceration for non-violent offenders and the relationship
between drug use, drug sales and drug arrests. For example,
Mauer observes that Blacks comprise 49% of those arrested for
drug sales, although most drug dealers are White.

McCain, Tracey L. (1992). The interplay of editorial and
   prosecutorial discretion in the perpetuation of racism in the

criminal justice system. Columbia Journal of Law and Social Problems, 25 (4), 601-644.

Due to the prevalence of conscious and unconscious racism in the U.S. criminal justice system, the ability to provide a fair trial for African American defendants is severely hampered. This problem is exacerbated by the oft-times sensational media coverage of crime. As a result, racism is perpetuated throughout the various stages of the criminal case. The author argues that to eliminate racism, safeguards must be put in place, before case processing begins.

McIntyre, Charshee C. L. (1993). Criminalizing a race: Free Blacks during slavery. Queens, NY: Kayode.

Explanation of the historical processes through which slavery evolved and how Blacks were singled out for such treatment, text traces the creation of a social structure for Whites and enslaved Blacks. Author notes the first choice of founding fathers was to colonize free Blacks outside of their new White republic. This, however, proved too expensive. Consequently, prisons began to serve as the alternative. Based upon this historical overview, author concludes there is a direct link to contemporary prison racial patterns.

McKee, James B. (1993). Sociology and the race problem: The failure of a perspective. Chicago: University of Illinois Press.

Tracing developments in the sociology of race relations from the 1920s to the 1960s, text examines the underlying sociological perspective on race in American life and in the discipline's demeaning image of Blacks. Author contends that the failure of mainstream sociology to meaningfully critique race relations could be attributed to the dominant beliefs, values, and assumptions. Specifically, the American sociological perspective is a direct reflection of its creators, White sociologists.

Meares, Tracey L. (1998). Social organization and drug law
    enforcement. American Criminal Law Review, 35 (2), 191-
    227.

    Essay presents analysis and critique of drug law enforcement
    and policy and their impact on poor Black communities.
    Author provides overview of social organization theory and its
    impact upon current criminal justice policies.   Meares
    determines that a community-based social organization model,
    one which includes social programs and effective law
    enforcement, is necessary to address crime in poor minority
    communities. Specifically, Meares rejects incarceration as an
    anti-drug crime strategy; favors community-based policies,
    such   as   enhanced   partnerships   between   police   and
    communities; and argues for more effective anti-drug policing
    strategies, such as reverse-stings and loitering ordinances.

Miller, Jerome G. (1996). Search and destroy: African-American
    males in the criminal justice system.   Cambridge, MA:
    Cambridge University Press.

    Author presents historical and contemporary look at the role of
    race in the criminal justice system. Miller explores the origins
    of race-driven research which was designed to "prove" Black
    inferiority. He uses The Bell Curve to analyze how this racial
    research has evolved.   Miller discusses the political
    implications of this research and how crime policies --
    particularly the War on Drugs -- have been affected. Text
    includes historical and contemporary table data on rates of
    arrest and incarceration by race.

Oliver, William. (1994). The violent social world of Black men.
    New York: Lexington Books.

    Based upon detailed interviews with 41 Black men, who have
    been involved in violent confrontations and arguments.
    Confrontations include intraracial violence between Black men

in bars and bar settings. Findings used to analyze circumstances, precipitating events, and causes of violence by Black males. Oliver concludes that interpersonal violence by Black males is produced by multiple causes. It is concluded that structural reforms should be combined with community-based coalitions to prevent violence, schools for Black males should be established, and community policing should be implemented. Interview instrument included in appendix.

Patterson, James T. (1995). Race relations and the "Underclass" in modern America: Some historical observations. Qualitative Sociology, 18 (2), 237-261.

Three debates concerning U.S. race relations and the underclass are reviewed. Collectively, they address the changing perception of poor Black neighborhoods, the concept of the underclass and its causes, and the impact these debates have had on opinions and public policies. Slavery, Black community development following emancipation, Northern migration, welfare, employment, and racism are discussed.

Peak, Ken. (1997). African Americans in policing. In Roger G. Dunham, & Geoffrey P. Alpert (Eds.), Critical issues in policing: Contemporary readings (pp.356-362). Prospect Heights, IL: Waveland Press.

Article traces the development of African Americans in law enforcement. Author includes a discussion on the unequal treatment and marginality that Black police experience. Peak addresses reasons police agencies need to diversify the rank and file, through both recruitment and promotion of minority police officers. Specifically, increase diversity among the general population, provide role models for young minorities who contemplate a career in law enforcement, and promote a more democratic society. Further, the challenges to minority recruitment are discussed.

Poussaint, Alvin F. (1983). Black-on Black homicide: A
psychological-political perspective. Victimology, 8, 161-169.

Article explores the reasons for the high rate of Black
homicide. Specifically, Poussaint explores psychological
explanations for understanding why Black homicide rates are
7-8 times higher than White homicide rates. Author concludes
it is necessary to examine negative psychological dynamics,
including low self-esteem, self-hatred, and how these affect
crime rates for Blacks. Article also considers the impact of
death penalty and skin tone on sentencing patterns.

Reuter, Peter, Robert MacCoun, & Patrick Murphy. (1990). Money
from crime: A study of the economics of drug dealing in
Washington D.C. Santa Monica, CA: Rand.

A detailed evaluation of the economic impact of drug-related
crime on Washington, D.C. Data culled from 11,430 cases
involving defendants charged with drug dealing between 1985-
1987. Most of these are young Black men. This period
represents a peak in the crackdown on drug-dealing in the
District of Columbia. Most drug sales were for cocaine (crack
and/or powder). Study indicates that when compared with
other offenders, drug sellers are less likely to have completed
high school; are as likely to have other legal employment; and
earn higher hourly incomes than they can from legitimate
activites.

Richie, Beth E. (1996). Compelled to crime: The gender entrapment
of battered Black women. New York: Routledge.

Text explores how battered Black women who commit crime
are treated by the criminal justice system. Richie explores the
confluence of factors which create unique problems for Black
women who face abusive partners. She labels this
phenomenon "gender entrapment"--a paradigm which links
gender-identity development, violence against women, and

involvement in crime. Life-history interviews and focus groups with African American women at Rikers Island Correctional Facility, serve as basis for the research.

Roscigno, Vincent J., & Marino A. Bruce. (1995). Racial inequality and social control: Historical and contemporary patterns in the U.S. South. Sociological Spectrum, 15 (3), 323-349.

Authors explore theoretical underpinnings of research explaining disproportionate crime, arrest, and incarceration of African Americans. They conclude that most analyses focus on cultural and structural differences between racial groups, while overlooking key race and class factors. They offer a new model which evaluates the impact of race and class antagonisms and subordination. Authors note that it is important that racial research, particularly studies focused on the South, address these factors. Findings indicate racial competition increases African American arrest, because it affects employment opportunities. Also, findings support the need for research which considers local racial politics and its impact.

Rose, Harold M., & Paula D. McClain. (1990). Race, place and risk: Black homicide in urban America. Albany, NY: State University of New York Press.

Text focuses on nature, causes, and varieties of Black homicide. Chapter topics explore several issues, including Black females and lethal violence; victimization risks for Black males; weapons involved in homicides; societal, cultural and individual risk factors for Black homicide; and justice system processing of Black homicide cases. Authors conclude by considering the future implications of current trends.

Sampson, Robert J. (1987). Urban Black violence - The effect of male joblessness and family disruption. American Journal of

Sociology, 93 (2), 348-382.

Article examines relationship between crime, unemployment, and family instability within economically deprived Black communities. Author utilizes race-specific robbery and homicide rates to test the hypothesis that the effect of unemployment among adult Black males on crime is mediated by its effects on instability in the home. Sampson concludes that the evidences does not support a race-based criminogenic perspective. Rather, disproportionate Black involvement in crime is a reflection of high levels of economic instability in urban communities.

Sasson, Theodore. (1995). African American conspiracy theories and the social construction of crime. Sociological Inquiry, 65 (3-4), 265-285.

Article examines conspiracy theories about crime, drugs, and violence expressed by African Americans. The perception that crime and violence in Black communities is attributed to the actions of powerful Whites is discussed. Interviews were conducted with residents of a Black community in Boston. Author explores the prevalence and persistence of conspiracy theories in peer group discussions.

Schatzberg, Rufus, & Robert J. Kelly. (1997). African-American organized crime: A social history. New Brunswick, NJ: Rutgers University Press.

Examination of the social history of organized crime in general, and specifically within the African-American community. Authors argue that the constrictions of racism and economic deprivation foster organized crime. Text provides an overview of African American history and urban migration in relation to crime, the formation of an underground economy, drug and vice organizations, and how these phenomena relate to present day gangs.

Shihadeh, Edward S., & Nicole Flynn. (1996). Segregation and crime: The effect of Black isolation on the rates of Black urban violence. Social Forces, 74 (4), 1325-1352.

Using race-disaggregated U.C.R. data and 1990 census data for 151 U.S. cities, authors explore the conceptual link between segregation and crime. Specifically, they examine whether the social isolation of urban Blacks increases Black violence and measure the spatial isolation between Blacks and Whites. Black isolation emerged as a strong predictor of Black violence rates in major U.S. cities.

Smith, J. Clay Jr. (1994). Justice and jurisprudence and the Black lawyer. Notre Dame Law Review, 69 (5), 1077-1113.

Detailed overview of how Blackness was addressed in the body of the U.S. Constitution. Smith also details laws enacted to control Black movement during slavery. Excerpts from the slave codes of more than ten Southern states are included. These codes outline various punishments, including the sanctions slaves were to receive for attempting to read or escape, and those for Whites who sought to teach slaves how to read. Code sections also address the severity of punishment slaves were to receive for crimes, and their incapacity to serve as witnesses and jurors in cases involving Whites.

Taslitz, Andrew E. (1998). An African-American sense of fact: The O.J. trial and Black judges on justice. Public Interest Law Journal, 7 (2), 219-249.

Article explores ways in which African-Americans assess evidence, determine facts, and evaluate justice. Taslitz outlines what he labels as an "African-American sense of fact." The foundation of his argument is based upon indepth interviews with Black judges (from Linn Washington's book Black Judges on Justice). Based on these findings, Taslitz presents several theses, including Blacks take a holistic approach to determinations of character contrary to Whites; Blacks are more likely to hold skeptical views of law enforcement; and further, Blacks believe they have unequal assess to competent representation and unbiased juries in the criminal justice system. Author concludes that outlining this alternative sense of fact helps explain how different groups of people viewing the same facts can reach markedly different conclusions.

Texeira, Mary Thierry. (1994). Challenging tradition: African-American women as law enforcement officers within the context of the United States criminal justice system (Doctoral dissertation, University of California, Riverside, 1994). Dissertation Abstracts International, 55 (12), 4001.

Case study focuses on 65 active and retired African-American women officers in a single police agency. Texeira explores why and how respondents entered law enforcement. Additionally, author examines the differences between the experiences of African-American women in policing and their White male, Black male, and White female counterparts.

Washington, Linn. (1994). Black judges on justice: Perspectives from the bench. New York: The New Press.

Based upon detailed interviews with 14 Black jurists, text provides forum for judges to discuss wide-range of issues, including race relations, childhood, courtroom experiences, relationships with colleagues, and criminal justice policies. Interviewees include Joe Brown, A. Leon Higginbotham Jr., Constance Baker Motley, Reggie Walton, and Bruce Wright.

Weatherspoon, Floyd. (1998). African American males and the law: Cases and materials. New York: University Press of America.

Overview of African American men and their disproportionate involvement in the criminal justice system. Text considers various sociological factors which contribute and exacerbate this problem, and what is being done to address it. Court cases, law review articles, statutes, and other materials are included. Subjects covered include racial discrimination within the justice system, media representations of Black males, police brutality, death penalty, and the racial impact of the Federal Sentencing Guidelines.

Welch, Susan, Michael Combs, & John Gruhl. Do Black judges make a difference? (1988). American Journal of Political Science, 32 (1), 126-136.

Article explores differences in sentencing decisions between Black and White judges. Sample is based on 3,418 adult felony cases in which 10 Black and 130 White judges made the sentencing decision. Findings reveal that Black jurists were more equitable in their decision to incarcerate Black and White defendants, while their White counterparts were somewhat less likely to sentence a White defendant to prison. However, when examining overall sentencing severity, the opposite was true. White judges were found to be more evenhanded when sentencing either a Black or White defendant. Black judges, however, were found to treat Black defendants more leniently.

Wilbanks, William. (1987). The myth of a racist criminal justice system. Monterey, CA: Brooks/Cole Publishing.

Text provides overview of the literature on the role of race in the criminal justice system. Author first addresses how contemporary definitions of racism overlap with concepts of prejudice and discrimination and how these definitions greatly differ between Blacks and Whites. Wilbanks then reviews existing research to find evidence of discrimination by criminal justice personnel at each stage of the process. He concludes there is insufficient evidence to support a claim of systemic racism directed against Blacks.

Wilson, William Julius. (1996). When work disappears: The
    world of the new urban poor. New York: Random House.

    Text provides detailed exploration of the availability of
    employment in the nation's urban centers. Findings were based
    upon three studies, including the Urban Poverty and Family
    Life Study. Residents, employers, and employees contribute
    to Wilson's research on the impact of work opportunities on
    quality of life for lower-class, Black Chicago residents.
    Wilson finds among other things: residents who are eager to
    find work; potential employees who have inadequate market
    skills; and employers who are suspicious of potential
    employees who live in low-income areas. After concluding
    that the greatest socio-cultural threat to Blacks in the inner-city
    is the decline in urban center jobs, Wilson makes several
    policy recommendations.

Young, Vernetta, & Anne Thomas Sulton. (1991). Excluded: The
    status of African-American scholars in the field of criminology
    and criminal justice. Journal of Research in Crime and
    Delinquency, 28 (1), 101-116.

    Article provokes thoughtful dialogue about the perspectives of
    African-American criminologists, the extent to which they
    have been excluded from the field of criminology and criminal
    justice, and methods by which they can be included in efforts
    to reduce crime and delinquency. Authors encourage scholars
    and policy makers to include the perspectives advanced by
    African-American criminologists.

II

GENERAL RACE RESEARCH

Part 6

Multi-Racial

Applegate, Brandon, John Wright, R. Gregory Dunway, Francis T. Cullen, & John D. Wooldredge. (1993). Victim-offender race and support for capital punishment: A factorial design approach. American Journal of Criminal Justice, 18 (1), 95-115.

Factorial design method is used to examine role race plays in capital punishment. Authors employed vignettes which portrayed various racial combinations of victims and offenders. Analyses indicate that race of the offender, not the victim, significantly influenced support for capital punishment. It is concluded that procedural safeguards alone may not eliminate racial bias in capital sentencing.

Arthur, John, & Charles Case. (1994). Race, class and support for police use of force. Crime, Law and Social Change, 21 (2), 167-182.

Study investigates public attitudes toward use of force by police officers through a re-analysis of data from a nationwide sample taken in 1991. Study indicates that members of groups with greater power, status, and advantages (Whites, males, highly educated, and wealthy), are more likely to favor police use of force than members of less privileged groups. In 1991,

70 percent of Whites and 43 percent of Blacks approved of a "policeman striking an adult male citizen" under some circumstances.

Baldus, David, George Woodworth, & Charles Pulaski. (1990). Equal justice and the death penalty: A legal and empirical analysis. Boston: Northeastern University Press.

Review of Georgia death sentencing patterns since *Furman v. Georgia* (1972). Data from Georgia courts and corrections department were analyzed to compare pre and post-*Furman* cases (over 2,000) that resulted in murder convictions, between 1973 and 1978. Multiple regression analysis, which controlled for more than 230 variables, was used. Researchers found that race of the victim was a significant predictor for death sentences. Defendants with White victims, particularly Black defendants, were most likely to be sentenced to death. Black defendants who killed Whites, were seven times more likely than White defendants who killed Blacks to receive the death penalty. Authors argue for limiting death penalty to only the most egregious crimes, to decrease the race effect.

Barak, Gregg. (1991). Cultural literacy and multicultural inquiry into the study of crime and justice. Journal of Criminal Justice Education, 2 (2), 173-192.

Examination of the development and use of cultural literacy in criminology and criminal justice curriculum. Author argues that while such discourse is presented as a means to bridge the communication gap between racial and ethnic groups, it fails to overcome the traditional definitions of crime and the administration of justice. Barak surveys and critiques the existing literature and offers seminal readings which expand African American literacy in criminology.

Barlow, David E. (1994). Minorities policing minorities as a strategy of social control: A historical analysis of tribal police in the United States. In Louis A. Knafla (Ed.), Criminal justice history: An international annual. Vol. 15 (pp.141-163). Westport, CT: Greenwood Press.

Study contrasts the development of Indian tribal police with the contemporary use of African American officers to police predominantly Black neighborhoods. While such practices are presented as evidence of a more representative and progressive criminal justice system, author contends such actions serve as an additional means of enhancing social control over subordinate populations. Minority hiring practices and the lack of institutional reforms are also discussed.

Barlow, Melissa Hickman, & David E. Barlow. (1995). Confronting ideologies of race and crime in the classroom: The power of history. Journal of Criminal Justice Education, 6 (1), 105-122.

Critique of ideologies related to crime and race. Specifically, authors explore how race, notably Blackness, is represented in the criminal justice classroom. Article includes discussion of authors' experiences teaching racial issues at both predominantly White colleges and historically Black institutions. They conclude that "historical multiculturalism" should be part of criminal justice education. This perspective, which provides a historical backdrop for discussions of race, helps students to "recognize ideologies as ideologies" and thereby enables them to critique them.

Barlow, Melissa Hickman, David E. Barlow, & Stan Stojkovic. (1994). The media, the police and the multicultural community: Observations on a city in crisis. Journal of Crime and Justice, 17 (2), 133-165.

Examines media treatment of events surrounding the 1991 Jeffrey Dahmer serial murder case in Milwaukee. Specifically, the aftermath following the decision by police officers to return a young Laotian boy to Dahmer's custody after concluding the incident was nothing more than a domestic dispute between homosexual lovers. The end consequence of this decision was the boy's death. Data were gathered from newspaper articles appearing in the city's two main papers; articles from alternative and community newspapers; conversations with members of the fire and police commission; and information gathered through attendance at public police forums. Authors argue media treatment of the incident failed to address the broader political and economic relations that are present between different social strata in the community.

Barnes, Carole W., & Rodney Kingsworth (1996). Race, drugs, and criminal sentencing: Hidden effects of the criminal law. Journal of Criminal Justice, 24 (1), 39-55.

Article explores the interaction between offenders' racial background, drug involvement, and criminal justice system processing. Data were derived from 1,379 cases involving individuals arrested and charged with a single drug felony in Sacramento, California, between 1987 and 1989. Findings demonstrate that Black offenders had their cases rejected or dismissed significantly more often than White or Latino offenders. Further, Whites were more likely to have their charges reduced and placed in a diversion program, while Blacks were most likely of the three groups to be sentenced to prison. Authors conclude that the nature of specific drug markets, along with current law enforcement strategies of drug control, account for noted racial differences.

Bing, Robert, Chinita Heard, & Evelyn Gilbert. (1995). The experiences of African Americans and Whites in criminal justice education: Do race and gender differences exist?" Journal of Criminal Justice Education, 4 (1), 123-141.

Researchers examine the differences in the experiences between African American and White students in criminal justice education. Analysis and discussion of gender and race discrimination in academia indicate that women and minorities have markedly different experiences. Authors conclude that further research on gender and racial biases in criminal justice academia is necessary.

Bishop, Donna M., & Charles E. Frazier. (1996). Race effects in juvenile justice decision-making: Findings of a statewide analysis. Journal of Criminal Law and Criminology, 86 (2), 392-414.

State-wide examination of how race impacts juvenile court decisions. Data set includes the total population of youths (161,369) referred to Florida's juvenile intake from 1985 to 1987. These cases include referrals for both delinquent acts and status offenses. Logistic regression used to estimate case processing models that control for legal variables. Analysis indicates that non-White juveniles are disadvantaged at several stages of case processing. Non-White youths, for instance, are more likely to be recommended for petition to court, to be held in detention (prior to case adjudication), and are more likely to be formally processed, than comparable White youths. Research findings also include an interview component. Telephone interviews were conducted with a random sample of 34 juvenile justice officials.

Blumstein, Alfred. (1982). On the racial disproportionality of United States' prison populations. Journal of Criminal Law and Criminology, 73, 1259-1281.

Article explores the disproportionately high rate of incarceration for Blacks as compared with Whites. Blumstein evaluates whether racial discrimination or disproportionate offending explains this disparity. Using 1970s data on the state prison population, distribution of offenses, and arrest data by race, Blumstein concludes that 80 percent of the racial disparity in incarceration is explained by differential racial patterns of arrest.

Blumstein, Alfred. (1993). Racial disproportionality of U.S. prison populations revisited. University of Colorado Law Review, 64 (3), 743-760.

Article revisits Blumstein's earlier arguments which assess the rationale for the racial composition of U.S. prisons. In 1983, he found that approximately 80 percent of racial disproportionality in prison was explained by differential arrest rates for index offenses. It was concluded that these differentials explain racial disproportionality in incarceration rates. An update of this analysis indicates that about 76 percent of racial disproportionality is explained by arrest rates. In addressing the remaining 24 percent, Blumstein concludes the cause is "not so much due to racial discrimination" but other factors, which contribute to limited opportunities for Blacks.

Bogus, Carl T. (1993). Race, riots, and guns. Southern California Law Review, 66 (4), 1365-1388.

A consideration of how White fear of Black crime has been used to increase gun ownership among Whites. Author evaluates advertisements used by the National Rifle Association following the 1992 Rodney King/L.A.P.D. riots. Analysis includes historical and contemporary overview of role race has played in gun ownership and gun control debates. Specifically, the goals of the Second Amendment are reviewed. Article concludes that strict gun control laws benefit society.

Bridges, George S., & Robert D. Crutchfield. (1988). Law, social standing and racial disparities in imprisonment. Social Forces, 66 (3), 699-724.

Study examines whether state and regional variables--social, economic and legal--impact racial disparity in imprisonment. Authors use state prison data, the Uniform Crime Reports, and information on crime patterns and legal factors for each state. Four findings: (1) There is wide-spread variation across states in their racial disparity in incarceration; (2) State laws have little impact upon racial disparity in prison; (3) State social characteristics significantly affect racial disparity; and (4) Arrest rates have less impact on racial disparity in prisons than previously hypothesized.

Brown, M. Craig, & Barbara D. Warner. (1992). Immigrants, urban politics, and policing in 1900. American Sociological Review, 57 (3), 293-305.

An exploration of how nonimmigrants responded to the influx of immigrant populations in urban areas. Research focuses on American cities in 1900 and finds that nonimmigrants perceived immigrants as undesirable and threatening. Pressure was placed on police to control these threatening populations and their "foreign" lifestyles, such as alcohol consumption. Authors test conflict theory's threat hypothesis and include political variables in their analysis. Findings indicate that political motivations explain aggressive police response to drunkenness in immigrant communities.

Browning, Sandra L., & Liqun Cao. (1993). The impact of race on criminal justice ideology. Justice Quarterly, 9 (4), 685-701.

Study examines whether race shapes individual perceptions of the criminal justice system. Utilizing data obtained via telephone interviews with 103 Black and 136 White Cincinnati residents, findings show race to be a significant predictor of criminal justice ideology, even after controlling for an individual's age, sex, education, and income. Specifically, Blacks were more likely than Whites to view society and the criminal justice system from a conflict perspective.

Burnett, Arthur L., Sr. (1994). Permeation of race, national origin and gender issues from initial law enforcement contact through sentencing: The need for sensitivity, equalitarianism and vigilance in the criminal justice system. American Criminal Law Review, 31 (4), 1153-1175.

Policy review examines the various stages of the criminal justice system at which racial, ethnic, and gender bias may be introduced. Author discusses the use of drug courier profiles by law enforcement, plea bargaining decisions by prosecutors, use of peremptory challenges during 'jury selection, and mandatory sentencing statutes. Burnett contends the issue is whether any of the aforementioned practices and policies are applied in a discriminatory manner or have unintended adverse consequences for minorities.

Cernkovich, Stephen, & Peggy Giordano. (1992). School bonding, age, race, and delinquency. Criminology, 30 (2), 261-291.

Utilizing data on 942 youths in the Toledo, Ohio metropolitan area, authors assess the efficacy of control theory in predicting delinquency by examining the degree to which respondents reported attachment to school. Researchers found Blacks were as strongly bonded to school as Whites. The control theory model explained much of the variance in delinquency across racial and gender subgroups. Also, racial composition of the school was not relevant in explaining the effect of school bonding on delinquency.

Chavez, Ernest, E. R. Oetting, & Randall Swaim. (1994). Dropout and delinquency: Mexican-American and Caucasian non-Hispanic youth. Journal of Clinical Child Psychology, 23 (1), 47-55.

Based upon sample of 1,637 from an urban area, a mid-sized community, and a small community in two Southwestern states, study examines delinquency patterns for White and

Mexican-American youths. Dropouts and students with poor grades were the groups most likely to engage in delinquent behaviors. Also, Mexican-American youths, across academic groups, were slightly less likely than Whites to engage in delinquency. Researchers suggest that the high delinquency rate for Mexican-Americans may be due to their high dropout rate.

Clarke, James W. (1998). The lineaments of wrath: Race, violent crime, and American culture. New Brunswick, NJ: Transaction Publishers.

Comprehensive overview of impact of race and violence in America over the past four centuries. Focusing on Whites and Blacks, text explores wide array of topics, including the violence of slavery, lynching, and early 20th century racial trends in homicide. Text also details various forms of racial oppression, such as the convict-lease system, disenfranchisement, and segregation. Clarke ultimately links this violent past with Black life in contemporary U.S. society.

Cole, David. (1999). No equal justice: Race and class in the American criminal justice system. New York: New Press.

Book provides historical and contemporary assessment of how the application of constitutional guarantees are affected by race and class. Legal and empirical review of racial profiling, right to counsel, jury selection, and sentencing indicates there is a double standard operating in the American criminal justice system. Cole finds that the justice system's race and class inequities are perpetuated by U.S. Supreme Court decisions which rest on "race-neutrality."

Connolly, Kathleen, Lea McDermid, Vincent Schiraldi, & Dan Macallair. (1996). From classrooms to cell blocks: How prison building affects higher education and African American enrollment. San Francisco: Center on Juvenile & Criminal

Justice.

Report looks at how California's prison construction has affected the state's Black population. Since 1980, there has been an eight-fold increase in the state's prison budget, making prison more accessible than higher education for African Americans. Report notes the following: 1,922 in every 100,000 African Americans are in prison, compared with 236 in every 100,000 for Whites; 27, 207 African Americans attend public four-year universities, while 44,792 are behind bars. Based on findings, five recommendations are made, including the need for a moratorium on prison construction.

Cullen, Francis T., Liqun Cao, James Frank, Robert H. Langworthy, Sandra L. Browning, Renee Kopache, & Thomas J. Stevenson. (1996). "Stop or I'll shoot": Racial differences in support for police use of deadly force. American Behavioral Scientist, 39 (4), 449-460.

Survey data on 103 Black and 136 White Cincinnati residents were used to explore the impact of race on support for police use of deadly force against fleeing felons. Consistent with U.S. Supreme Court decision in *Tennessee v. Garner* (1985), both groups' approval of force was high when offenders manifested "past dangerousness." Less support, however, was found for use of deadly force where offenders committed non-violent crimes. Authors also found that Blacks were less likely than Whites to endorse the inappropriate use of deadly force.

Curry, G. David, & Irving Spergel. (1992). Gang involvement and delinquency among Hispanic and African-American adolescent males. Journal of Research in Crime and Delinquency, 29 (3), 273-291.

Article examines gang involvement and delinquency among Hispanic and African-American males, in Chicago public schools. In 1987, researchers surveyed 139 Hispanic and 300

African-American boys in the sixth through eighth grade. Findings reveal that gang involvement and delinquency among Hispanic youth are closely associated with intra-personal variables. For African-American youths, however, involvement is more closely associated with social and inter-personal variables.

Daly, Kathleen, & Michael Tonry. (1997). Gender, race, and sentencing. In Michael Tonry (Ed.), Crime and justice: A review of research: Vol.22 (pp.201-252). Chicago: University of Chicago Press.

Review examines how race and gender are conceptualized in sentencing in the criminal justice process. The empirical research reveals that Black males may be more likely than either White men or women of any race to benefit from limited discretion and limited individualization of sentencing. However, Black and White women may be more likely to benefit from broader discretion and greater individualization.

Dannefer, Dale, & Russell Schutt. (1982). Race and juvenile justice processing in court and police agencies. American Journal of Sociology, 87 (5), 1113-1131.

Study evaluates bias in the juvenile justice system. The data are used to analyze two factors which impact bias; the characteristics and procedural constraints of processing agencies; and the characteristics of their social environments. Using juvenile case dispositions in two New Jersey counties, researchers find there is a greater probability of race-based bias in police dispositions than in judicial decision-making.

Davis, Angela J. (1998). Prosecution and race: The power and privilege of discretion. Fordham Law Review, 67 (1), 13-68.

Detailed legal analysis of how race impacts prosecutorial decisions. Author examines the gateway role prosecutors have in the criminal justice system, how race affects their practices, and how the absence of adequate checks and balances against prosecutorial misconduct impacts justice system legitimacy. Davis uses critique of case law, including *U.S. v. Armstrong* (1996), to buttress argument that race affects prosecutorial practices. It is concluded that prosecution offices should use racial impact studies to promote the non-discriminatory use of prosecutorial discretion.

Davis, Christopher, Richard Estes, & Vincent Schiraldi. (1996). Three strikes: The new apartheid. San Francisco: Center on Juvenile & Criminal Justice.

Report examines effect of three strikes legislation on California's offender population and its criminal justice system. Particular focus on the African American offender population. Data reveal that Blacks, who comprise 7 percent of state population, account for 43 percent of those sentenced under three strikes law. Authors conclude such legislation has reinforced punitive and racially disparate policies and should be abolished.

Davis, Peter L. (1994). Rodney King and the decriminalization of police brutality in America: Direct and judicial access to the grand jury as remedies for victims of police brutality when the prosecutor declines to prosecute. Maryland Law Review, 53 (2), 271-357.

Drawing from the Rodney King incident, author contends that police brutality has been *de facto* decriminalized in the U.S., particularly when incidents involve minority victims. Minority attitudes toward police continue to deteriorate as sanctions (e.g., civil suits and civilian review boards) continue to be ineffective in stemming police abuse. Davis argues that the power to bring charges against offending officers should not rest solely with prosecution. Rather, efforts should be re-directed toward empowering citizens. Authors recommend citizen access to the grand jury.

Dudley, William (Ed.). (1991). Police brutality. San Diego, CA: Greenhaven Press.

Edited volume of essays on police brutality. Articles address broad range of issues, including impact of police abuse on minority communities, juveniles, and the poor. Text explores a variety of reforms that have been proposed to stem the rise in brutality claims. Contributors include William Bratton, David Dinkins, James Fyfe, George Kelling, Joseph Kennedy, and Jerome Skolnick.

Duster, Troy. (1997). Pattern, purpose, and race in the drug war: The crisis of credibility in criminal justice. In Craig Reinarman & Harry G. Levine (Eds.), Crack in America: Demon drugs and social justice (pp.260-287). Berkeley, CA: University of California Press.

Based on testimony given before the U.S. House of Representatives, chapter discusses punitive effects the War on Drugs has had on minorities and the poor. Author argues that the War on Drugs' negative impact has gone beyond its exclusive focus on street level drug enforcement. It has also detrimentally affected the economy in the inner city. Author examines the subsequent switch from an industrial to a service-industry and the impact such changes have had on the lives of minority youths.

Eisenman, Russell. (1995). Is there bias in U.S. law enforcement? Journal of Social, Political and Economic Studies, 20 (2), 229-240.

Differences in criminal behavior among Blacks and Whites in the U.S. are examined through an analysis of 1991 national data from the F.B.I. Analysis reveals a disproportionately high rate of Black arrests for U.C.R. offenses even after controlling

for demographics for both juvenile and adult offenders.
Validity and interpretation of these data and claims of law
enforcement bias are discussed.

Elion, Victor H., & Edwin E. Megargee. (1979). Racial identity,
length of incarceration, and parole decision making. Journal
of Research in Crime and Delinquency, 16 (2), 233-245.

Longitudinal study of racial disparity in sentencing patterns for
Blacks and Whites. Inmate sample of 1,345 was drawn from
the Federal Correctional Institution, between 1970-1974.
Thirteen offender variables were used, focusing on personal
and social factors, legal case characteristics, and institutional
adjustment measures. Among the findings: Black inmates
served much longer proportions of their initial sentences than
White inmates; and Whites were significantly more likely to
receive parole. Discriminant analyses indicate that parole
primarily determined by initial sentence term. Authors
conclude that race may operate as a "surrogate variable" for
complicated social-structural interactions.

Elliot, Delbert S., & Suzanne S. Ageton. (1980). Reconciling race
and class differences in self-reported and official estimates of
delinquency. American Sociological Review, 45 (1), 95-110.

Evaluation of gap in delinquency reports between self-report
data and official estimates. Authors outline critique of self-
report measures, including representations of items, ambiguity
in responses, and administration of self-report studies. This is
followed by a discussion and application of new approaches to
self-report methods, compared with official estimates.

Eron, Leonard D., Jacquelyn H. Gentry, & Peggy Schlegel (Eds.).
(1994). Reason to hope: A psychological perspective on
violence and youth. Washington, DC: American Psychological
Association.

Text presents a continuum of social, individual, and contextual factors in exploring the etiology of violence; violence among different racial, ethnic (e.g., African-Americans, American Indians, and Hispanics), and vulnerable populations; social influences on youth violence; preventive and treatment interventions; and research and policy recommendations.

Farr, Kathryn Ann. (1997). Aggravating and differentiating factors in the case of White and minority women on death row. Crime and Delinquency, 43 (3), 260-278.

Research analyzes 35 cases of women on death row in 1993. The most aggravated cases involved White women who were implicated in multiple killings of White victims. Overall, the murders committed by women of color were less likely to be aggravated than those committed by Whites and were motivated by revenge or anger. Most of the murders examined in this study were intra-racial.

Ferguson, Florence Sylvia. (1996). Race, urbanism, and court bureaucratization: An empirical examination of conflict-Weberian theories (Doctoral dissertation, Michigan State University, 1996). Dissertation Abstracts International, 58 (1), 298.

Drawing from a conflict-Weberian perspective, study examines relationship between race, urbanism, and court bureaucracy. Conflict theorists argue that Black offenders receive harsher sentences than Whites because of their subordinate status in society, whereas the Weberian perspective views courts as bureaucracies, with efficiency being the most important organizational goal. Drawing from a Pennsylvania sample of convicted felons, study measures effects of race, urbanization, and court bureaucratization on probability of incarceration. Findings support conflict perspective, but only with male offenders. Specifically, Black males were more likely to be incarcerated than all other offenders.

Finkelman, Paul. (1993). The crime of color. Tulane Law Review, 67 (6), 2063-2112.

Article reviews historical origins of the association between Blackness and criminality. Article provides detailed discussion of how the slave codes created racial double standards, punishing Blacks for activity which would be legal if committed by Whites. Finkelman looks at colonial-era laws in Virginia, Maryland, and South Carolina and finds that they were used as means of social control, economic exploitation, and class stratification. Article also considers how other minority groups, such as American Indians and Asian Americans, historically fared under U.S. law.

Flowers, Ronald Barri. (1990). Minorities and criminality. New York: Praeger.

A wide-ranging look at offending and victimization patterns for racial and ethnic minorities. Text evaluates interracial and race-specific theories of minority offending. Specifically, Flowers reviews the empirical literature on Blacks, Hispanics, Native Americans. As well, text reviews differential law enforcement, incarceration, and minority involvement in organized crime. Flowers concludes with an overview of how issues of minorities and criminal justice should be addressed in legislation, criminal justice curriculum, and research.

Foley, Linda A., Afesa M. Adams, & James L. Goodson, Jr. (1996). The effect of race on decisions by judges and other officers of the court. Journal of Applied Social Psychology, 26 (13), 1190-1212.

Utilizing a sample of judges, attorneys, and probation officers, the authors present a series of nine trial vignettes of an aggravated, interracial robbery case. Authors examine whether the racial background of both the defendant and victim impact the perceptions of criminal justice officials, and how they subsequently handle the case. Attorneys (prosecuting and defense), and probation officers considered the White defendant to be the more serious offender. Judges, however, considered minority offenders who victimized someone White to be more likely to recidivate.

Fukurai, Hiroshi, Edgar W. Butler, & Richard Krooth. (1993). Race and the jury. New York: Plenum.

Text reviews the effects of race on juries in the U.S. Using both historical and contemporary court records, authors examine the institutional and structural mechanisms in society that have prevented adequate representation of racial and ethnic minorities from serving on juries. Also addressed are the methodological challenges often present in those studies evaluating racial representation in juries.

Gibson, James L. (1978). Race as a determinant of criminal sentences: A methodological critique and a case study. Law and Society Review, 25 (2), 200-218.

Examination of racial discrimination research in criminal courts in the United States. Past research emphasizes discrimination as a function of societal forces rather than an attribute of individual decision makers. This produces research designs that analyze decisions of courts rather than decisions of individual judges. A finding of no discrimination does not eliminate the possibility that judges rule in favor or against minorities. Using data drawn from the Georgia Fulton County Superior Court, from 1968-1970, it was found that anti-Black judges are strongly tied to traditional Southern culture, are prejudiced against Blacks, and punitive in sentencing.

Goldkamp, John S. (1976). Minorities as victims of police shootings:

Interpretations of racial disproportionality and police use of deadly force. The Justice System Journal, 2 (2), 169-183.

Article examines the problem of police shootings of minority citizens. Author notes that this form of the "death penalty" does not have the same due process safeguards that are available for a post-conviction sentence of death. Two explanations -- police targeting and disproportionate minority involvement in crime -- are offered for the disproportionate rate of police-minority shootings. Author concludes that these perspectives provide a good starting point for analyzing the problem. Additional study should explore the role of class and how race and class may be interrelated.

Greenberg, Michael, & Dona Schneider. (1994). Violence in American cities: Young Black males is the answer, but what was the question? Social Science Medicine, 39 (2), 179-187.

An empirical test of whether the problem of violence can be addressed by focusing on young African American males. Authors study three medium-sized, "marginal" New Jersey cities (Camden, Newark, and Trenton), to determine rates of violence. For all three cities, violent death rates for Whites, Hispanics, and Blacks were similar. Based upon these findings, compared with rates for other cities, researchers conclude that problem of marginalization must be addressed to reduce urban violence.

Gryski, Gerard S., Gary Zuk, & Deborah J. Barrow. (1994). A bench that looks like America? Representation of African Americans and Latinos on the Federal Courts. The Journal of Politics, 56 (4), 1076-1086.

Study explores whether political and socio-economic determinants, identified in research on state and local representation, explain appointments of African Americans and Latinos to the federal bench. Data from the 1970-1990 census, state and national political directories were used to create socio-economic and political profiles for 90 of the 94 U.S. judicial districts. Findings indicate that political and demographic factors explain African American recruitment to the bench, while socio-economic factors explain Latino recruitment.

Hacker, Andrew. (1995). Two nations: Black and White, separate, hostile, unequal. New York: Ballantine.

Text discusses and explores reasons for the tense relationship between Blacks and Whites in contemporary U.S. society. Hacker considers the historical origins of these conflicts. Author combines personal observations with data on crime, education, housing, and employment. Text concludes that more open discussion and reforms are necessary to bridge the U.S. racial gap.

Hagan, John, & Ruth D. Peterson. (1995). Criminal inequality in America: Patterns and consequences. In John Hagan, & Ruth D. Peterson (Eds.), Crime and inequality (pp.14-36). Stanford, CA: Stanford University Press.

Research has demonstrated that violent crime in the U.S. is increasingly concentrated among young, disadvantaged, minority males. This is notably true for African Americans, Hispanics, and Native Americans. Chapter explores the relationship between crime and inequality in terms of intersections of race, gender, and economic status. Authors discuss the role that racial discrimination and segregation play in minority crime, the treatment of minorities in the criminal justice system, and interactions between minorities and justice officials.

Hagedorn, John. (1994). Neighborhoods, markets, and gang drug organization. Journal of Research in Crime and Delinquency, 31 (3), 264-294.

98 Race and Crime

Using data drawn from observations and fieldwork conducted in 1987 and 1992, study examines the sources of variation in the drug-selling organization of gangs from Milwaukee. Three-hour interviews were held with 101 founding members of 18 gangs. The study indicates that as sales to affluent Whites increase, more efficient drug-selling structures are created. Most White adult gang members sell cocaine in addition to their full time job, while Black adult gang members are more reliant on dealing as a primary source of income.

Harer, Miles D., & Darrell Steffensmeier. (1992). The differing effects of economic inequality on Black and White rates of violence. Social Forces, 70 (4), 1035-1054.

Analysis of the relationship between economic inequality and rates of White and Black violent crime. Standard Metropolitan Statistical Area (SMSA) data for 1980, disaggregated by race, are used. Impact of economic inequality shows marked differences for Whites and Blacks. For Whites, high inequality is associated with high arrest rates for violent crimes. For Blacks, however, inequality shows weak effect on arrests for violent crime. Authors conclude that data support structural explanations of Black rates of violence.

Harris, Anthony R. (1991). Race, class and crime. In Joseph Sheley (Ed.), Criminology: A contemporary handbook (pp. 95-119). Belmont, CA: Wadsworth Publishing Company.

Article examines intersections between race, class, and crime. Harris critiques ways in which official data and unofficial data are biased in terms of race and class. Specifically, he asserts, there is an inherent race and crime bias which skews criminological inquiry toward street crime and crime by the poor. Harris finds that even with this bias, there is still a race-crime relationship. Article then reviews some theoretical explanations of the race-street crime relationship, including social class, constitutional differences, family structure, and subculture. Harris rejects these and concludes that historical caste explains the race-crime relationship. At one end, Whites are overrepresented in white-collar crime and at the other, Blacks are overrepresented in street crime.

Harris, David A. (1998). Car wars: The Fourth Amendment's death on the highway. George Washington Law Review, 66 (3), 556-590.

Review and critique of three U.S. Supreme Court decisions on routine traffic stops of minority drivers: *Whren v. U.S.* (1996), *Ohio v. Robinette* (1996), and *Maryland v. Wilson* (1997). After a detailed discussion of these cases, Harris concludes that the Fourth Amendment guarantee against unreasonable searches and seizures is at risk for minority motorists. The purported goals of racial profiling, such as fighting the War on Drugs, are outweighed by its high costs, particularly civil litigation. Harris observes that when constitutional rights are compromised for some groups, it is only a matter of time before they will be compromised for society at large. Article includes proposals which would address problems associated with racial profiling.

Hawkins, Darnell F., John H. Laub, & Janet L. Lauritsen. (1998). Race, ethnicity, and serious juvenile offending. In Rolf Loeber, & David P. Farrington (Eds.), Serious & violent juvenile offenders: Risk factors and successful interventions (pp. 30-46). Thousand Oaks, CA: Sage.

The Uniform Crime Reports, self-reports, and victimization surveys are used to examine the relationship between race, ethnicity, and youth offending. Authors provide an overview of juvenile crime statistics by race, national and local trends in youth violence, and summarize the logitundinal research on chronic juvenile offending. Analysis includes information on Whites, Blacks, American Indians, Asian, and Hispanics. Authors explore reasons for the paucity of criminological attention to the role socio-economic factors play in explaining race differentials in offending. They conclude that theorizing should be expanded to include more aggregate-level crime correlates.

Henderson, Martha L., Francis T. Cullen, Liqun Cao, Sandra L. Browning, & Renee Kopache. (1997). Impact of race on perceptions of criminal injustice. Journal of Criminal Justice, 25 (6), 447-462.

Employing data derived from a stratified sample of 239 Cincinnati residents, study explores whether African Americans and Whites vary in their perceptions of racial injustice in the criminal justice system. Findings, reveal a difference, even after controlling for respondents socio-demographic characteristics, experience with the criminal justice system, and crime-related ideology. Further, viewpoints on injustice were most prevalent among poor African Americans.

Herrnstein, Richard J., & Charles Murray. (1994). The bell curve: Intelligence and class structure in American life. New York: Free Press.

Authors consider role of intelligence in American life. Text discusses of the "cognitive elite," addresses impact of intelligence and I.Q. test performance on crime, poverty, schooling, unemployment, civility, and parenting. Throughout text and on various topics, such as affirmative action, authors discuss race and ethnicity. They conclude that some racial groups are destined by their intelligence to certain fates.

Hindelang, Michael. (1978). Race and involvement in common law personal crimes. American Sociological Review, 43 (1), 93-109.

Article evaluates whether the disproportionately high rate of arrests for Blacks is the result of bias within the criminal justice system or disproportionate offending. Research focuses upon the following crimes: murder, rape, robbery, and assault ("common law personal crimes"). Author notes that earlier research on this issue is based on either self-report data or official data. Most of the research based on the self-report data found racial bias, while research based on the official data support differential involvement. Hindelang, using national victimization data to test the hypothesis, finds that most of the racial disproportionality in arrest is explained by disproportionately high rate of offending by Blacks.

Houts, Sandra, & Cathy Kassab. (1997). Rotter's social learning theory and fear of crime: Differences by race and ethnicity. Social Science Quarterly, 78 (1), 122-136.

Study tests Julian B. Rotter's (1996) social learning theory by examining racial and ethnic differences in fear of crime. Drawing on 1993 telephone survey data in a Midwestern city, sample included 518 adults -- 76 percent White, 16 percent Black and 8 percent Other. Findings indicate that social learning was better at explaining fear of crime for Whites than for non-Whites. Authors call for further research to examine what factors affect fear of crime in non-White populations.

Hunt, Geoffrey, Karen Joe, & Dan Waldorf. (1996). 'Drinking, kicking back and gang banging:' Alcohol, violence and street gangs. Free Inquiry--Special Issue: Gangs, Drugs & Violence, 24 (2), 123-132.

Article considers impact of drinking on street gang violence. Data based upon interview data from two studies on ethnic youth gangs in Northern California. Between 1990 and 1994, 659 gang members, from African American, Asian, and Hispanic communities were interviewed. Study focuses on both internal and external gang violence. Findings indicate that alcohol consumption is typically a precursor of aggressive

behavior. Authors conclude that future research should
continue to explore the role that drinking and violence have on
gang life.

Inciardi, James, Dorothy Lockwood, & Anne Pottieger. (1993).
Women and crack-cocaine. New York: Macmillan.

Text presents a compilation of material drawn from more than
4,000 pages of transcribed interviews with crack-addicted
African-American and White women. Data collected between
1985-1991, in Miami. Authors address why both social
policies and treatment options have generally failed to meet the
needs of this at-risk population.

Jackson, Jesse. (1996). Legal lynching: Racism, injustice and the
death penalty. New York: Marlowe.

Text provides detailed description of the history of capital
punishment and specifically focuses on the constitutional,
moral, and theological questions surrounding this practice.
Particular attention given to the impact of geography, race, sex,
and class on sentencing patterns and the application of the
death penalty in the United States.

Jackson, Pamela Irving. (1989). Minority group threat, crime, and
policing. New York: Praeger.

Study examines societal expectations for police work in the
United States. Data consisted of local, regional, and national
perspectives to identify conflicts within these expectations.
The central thesis is that mobilization of municipal police
resources in early 1970s was influenced by size of minority
population of a city. Factors such as socio-economic traits and
racial and ethnic population mix influenced expectations for
police officers and the support they received. The percentage
of Blacks and Hispanics in a population and Black-White
income inequality should be examined.

Jacobs, James B. (1979). Race relations and the prisoner subculture. In Norval Morris & Michael Tonry (Eds.), Crime and justice: An annual review of research: Vol.1 (pp.1-28). Chicago: University of Chicago Press.

Author contends that literature regarding race relations in prisoner subculture has been ignored despite the history of segregation and racial discrimination. Theories of prisoner subculture fail to consider racial factors. Prisoner subcultures are characterized by racial polarization and conflict and dominance of Blacks and other minorities who constitute most of the national prison population. Author suggests that research link the prison society, including its patterns of race relations, to both the unique characteristics of prisons and the culture and social structure of the larger society.

Jensen, Gary F., Joseph H. Strauss, & V. William Harris. (1977). Crime, delinquency, and the American Indian. Human Organization, 36 (3), 252-257.

Authors utilize national crime statistics to compare arrest rates among American Indians, Blacks, Asian Americans, and Whites. Analyses found American Indian rates far surpassed all other racial groups, particularly for alcohol-related offenses. Authors explore whether differences are attributed to socio-economic disadvantages experienced by Native Americans or cultural attitudes towards drinking.

Johnston, J. Philip. (1994). Academic approaches to race-crime statistics do not justify their collection. Canadian Journal of Criminology, 36 (2), 166-174.

Article reviews and challenges the influence of academic approaches on the collection of race-based crime statistics. Author contends that the rise of academic involvement in this area does not justify the collection of such information. Further, other variables are preferable to race. It is concluded

104 Race and Crime

that race-based statistics generally ignore the socially constructed nature of race. These data, therefore, are methodologically limited.

Kennedy, Randall. (1997). Race, crime, and the law. New York: Pantheon.

A detailed exploration of how race has shaped American criminal law. Author provides historical discussion of how the law has been used to control and limit constitutional guarantees for African-Americans. In Kennedy's discussion of race which focuses upon Blacks and Whites, he examines various contemporary issues involving race and the criminal justice system. Topics include race-based jury nullification, racial impact of drug laws and racial bias in the application of the death penalty. At the outset, Kennedy outlines four perspectives (e.g., law and order) which are used to frame racial-legal issues. These views are applied and critiqued throughout the text.

Kennedy, Stetson. (1990). Jim Crow guide: The way it was. Boca Raton, FL: Florida Atlantic University Press.

Indepth review of how U.S. law has been used to regulate and control minority populations. Text includes legislation aimed at Blacks, American Indians, Hispanics, and Asians. Detailed look at Jim Crow-era laws enacted to prevent minorities from excercising constitutional rights. Laws were designed to disenfranchise minorities and to prohibit interracial marriage. Stetson also discusses legislation which curtailed traveling, housing, and employment.

Kingery, Paul, Frank Biafora, & Rick Zimmerman. (1996). Risk factors for violent behaviors among ethnically diverse urban adolescents. School Psychology International, 17 (2), 171-188.

Based on a three year self-report study of 3,955 inner-city boys in junior high school, article examines violence among Miami youths. Study indicates that gun carrying at school is only slightly more prevalent among Blacks (6 percent) than among Whites (4 percent). White boys are more likely to carry knives than are Black adolescents. In addition, findings reveal that no single racial group is more violent than another.

Kleck, Gary. (1985). Life support for ailing hypotheses: Modes of summarizing the evidence for racial discrimination in sentencing. Law and Human Behavior, 9 (3), 271-285.

Detailed critique of research on racial discrimination in sentencing. Author lists five common practices used by researchers which skew research findings to indicate research support for finding racial discrimination. These include "selective citation," "letting the evidence speak for itself," "the mixed bag," and "research democracy" and "magnanimous neutrality." Kleck concludes that class is a greater predictor of sentencing than defendant's race.

Klein, Malcolm W. (1995). The American street gang: Its nature, prevalence, and control. New York: Oxford University Press.

Drawn from ethnographic research, author presents overview of sociological knowledge of street gangs in America. Text is organized around four issues: the definition of a gang; changes in gang behavior and activities; involvement of street gangs in drug dealing; and efficacy of community and law enforcement efforts at gang prevention and suppression. The prevalence of gangs in other countries is also examined.

Kleinman, Paula H., & Deborah S. David. (1973). Victimization and perception of crime in a ghetto community. Criminology, 11 (3), 307-343.

Study examines how race affects victimization and perceptions of crime. Sample included Blacks (British West Indian and

American-born), Puerto Ricans, and Whites. Findings based
upon 1971 interviews conducted by the National Opinion
Research Center. Other variables in the analysis include age,
sex, SES, religion, and length of residency. Findings indicate
comparable reports of victimization across race; postive
relationship between victimization and income; and perception
of crime comparable across sex.

Kleinman, Stephen P., Susan Turner, & Joan Petersilia. (1988).
    Racial equity in sentencing. Santa Monica, CA: Rand.

Re-analysis of the racial impact of California's Determinate
Sentencing Act (Petersilia, 1983). Data based on 11,553
criminal cases involving convictions for assault, robbery, theft,
burglary, forgery, or drug crimes. Based on 1980 cases
involving White, Latino, and Black defendants. Empirical
assessment of whether defendant received probation or
sentenced to prison. Findings indicate once there were
controls for crime, prior record, offender characteristics, and
process variables (e.g., type of counsel), there was no race
effect. Researchers conclude that the California sentencing
legislation may enhance racial equity in sentencing.

Knepper, Paul. (1996). Race, racism and crime statistics.
    Southern University Law Review, 24 (1), 71-111.

Article explores the public debate about the collection of race-
coded crime statistics. The discussion followed the
announcement by the Canadian Centre for Justice Statistics
that it would begin race-based collection for its revised
Uniform Crime Report program. The author examines the
usefulness of collecting official race-coded crime statistics in
the U.S. The following topics are addressed: the politics of
official race classification, the origins of race-coded crime
statistics, concerns about the value of race-crime statistics, and
the impact of a moratorium on official race-crime statistics.

LaFree, Gary, Kriss Drass, & Patrick O'Day. (1992). Race and
    crime in postwar America: Determinants of African-American
    and White rates, 1957-1988. Criminology, 30 (2), 157-188.

Time-series analysis based on 1957-1988 rates of robbery,
burglary and homicide. Study evaluates how Black and White
rates are affected by education, income, and family stability.
Researchers found that crime rates among Whites decline as
income and education increase. For Blacks, crime rates
increased with increases in income and education. Further, for
Blacks, crime decreased as percentage of female-headed
families increased.

LaFree, Gary, & Katheryn K. Russell. (1993). The argument for
    studying race and crime. Journal of Criminal Justice
    Education, 4 (2), 273-289.

Authors argue for studying race and crime in criminology and
criminal justice research and education. They provide a
history of race and criminology research in the U.S., pertinent
reasons for studying race and crime, and key concepts and
questions that should be considered in courses focusing on race
and crime issues. Discussion includes contemporary
representations of crime and race. Appendix cites notable
writings on crime and race.

Lasley, James R., & Michael K. Hooper. (1998). On racism and
    the L.A.P.D.: Was the Christopher Commission wrong?
    Social Science Quarterly, 79 (2), 378-389.

Using data derived from a random sample of approximately
2,800 officers, study examines perceptions of institutional
racism among Los Angeles Police Department officers.
Sample includes minority and White officers. Contrary to
previous findings reported by the Christopher Commission,
regression analyses indicate that minority officers register
higher approval ratings for the department than Whites.

Authors discuss findings in the theoretical context of police subcultures.

Laub, John H. (1983). Urbanism, race, and crime. Journal of Research in Crime and Delinquency, 20 (2),183-198.

Assessment of the affect of urbanism on crime. Evaluation of conventional criminological argument that urbanism is one of the most important correlates of crime. National Crime Survey data, 1973-1977 are used to test this relationship. Specifically, whether the presumed relationship still exists when race is introduced. Analysis indicates that once race is considered there is little variation in crime rate across different sized locales. Findings support a reconsideration of urbanism-crime link.

Lauritsen, Janet L., & Robert J. Sampson. (1998). Minorities, crime and criminal justice. In Michael Tonry (Ed.), The handbook of crime and punishment (pp.58-84). Oxford: Oxford University Press.

Comprehensive overview of research, including meta-analyses, on race and crime. Focus of summary is on empirical studies of Black and White offending and victimization patterns. Researchers present data, historical and contemporary, on how minorities fare in the justice system, theoretical explanations for disproportionate minority involvement in street crime, and implications for future research. Authors conclude that though racial discrimination exists in the criminal justice system, there is little evidence to support that it is either systematic or overt on the part of decisionmakers.

Lee, Seong-Sik. (1993). A cross-population test of social control and differential association theories of delinquency: Koreans, American Blacks, and American non-Blacks (Doctoral dissertation, The University of Wisconsin-Madison, 1993). Dissertation Abstracts International, 54 (9), 3601.

Author tests the relative efficacy of differential association and Travis Hirschi's social control theory, as applied to Korean and U.S. populations. Specifically, study examines whether cultural group differences may affect the generalizability of these theories and whether in a heterogeneous society, such as the U.S., differential association is more applicable to American Blacks and American non-Blacks. Findings failed to support either theory, irrespective of race. However, social bond was a stronger predictor of delinquency for Koreans than for African Americans or non-Blacks.

Lieber, Michael J. (1994). A comparison of juvenile court outcomes for Native Americans, African Americans, and Whites. Justice Quarterly, 11 (2), 257-279.

Study tests an interpretation of Max Weber's theory of decision-making through an examination of case processing of Whites, Blacks, and Native Americans in a juvenile court in the Midwest. Regression analysis was used to test whether Native American and Black juvenile offenders received harsher sanctions than their White counterparts and whether Native Americans were treated more harshly than White and Black juveniles. Findings support the first hypothesis, but not the second. Specifically, differential treatment varied with the stage of the proceedings, availability of court resources and youth's attitude.

Logan, John E., & Brian J. Stults. (1999). Racial differences in exposure to crime: The city and suburbs of Cleveland in 1990. Criminology, 37 (2), 251-276.

Exploration of how race impacts exposure to crime. Research based on analyis of Cleveland metropolitan region in 1990. Data from U.S. Census. Analysis of how home ownership, education, household income, age, sex, residential mobility, and occupation affect rates of violent and property crime. Findings indicate that White and Black suburbanites face much lower crime rates than comparable city residents; suburban Whites face a much lower crime threat than Black counterparts due to intra-suburban racial and income segregation; central city residents, across race and neighborhood, face comprable rates of property crime.

Long, Elton, et al. (1975). American minorities: The justice issue. Englewood Cliffs, NJ: Prentice Hall.

Authors explore impact of discrimination on Blacks and Native Americans. Using a socio-political-legal framework, the text addresses historical treatment of racial minorities in the U.S., civil rights struggles and protest, political trials, and discrimination in prison. Concludes with recommendations for improving police-minority community relations.

Lungren, Daniel E., & Mark L. Krotoski. (1995). Racial Justice Act of 1994: Undermining enforcement of the death penalty without promoting racial justice. University of Dayton Law Review, 20 (2), 655-697.

Article examines the proposed Racial Justice Act (R.J.A.) of 1994, specifically focusing on how it would affect the administration of the death penalty and criminal justice system. Presented as a legislative means to promote racial justice in the operation of the death penalty, the R.J.A. would allow capital defendants to present statistics from unrelated cases to demonstrate the role of race in capital sentencing decisions. Authors contend such legislation would undermine enforcement of the death penalty without promoting racial justice.

Lyon, Jean-Marie, Scott Henggeler, & James Hall. (1992). The family relations, peer relations, and criminal activities of Caucasian and Hispanic-American gang members. Journal of Abnormal Child Psychology, 20 (5), 439-449.

Study investigates the relationships among family and peer relations and the criminal activities of White and Hispanic gang members. The sample includes 131 incarcerated male juveniles who completed a battery of tests. Findings indicate higher rates of general delinquency and home-related delinquency (e.g., damage to family property, theft of family property) for Whites than for Hispanics.

Mann, Coramae Richey. (1993). Unequal justice: A question of color. Bloomington, IN: Indiana University Press.

Text provides detailed literature review on race and crime for Blacks, Hispanics, Native Americans, and Asian Americans. Author evaluates the difference between perceptions of minority involvement in crime and the reality of minority involvement in crime. Further, Mann explores how crime is defined and measured. Includes a comprehensive overview of key stages of criminal justice system processing, including police, courts, and corrections.

Martin, Susan E. (1994). 'Outside within' the station house: The impact of race and gender on Black women police. Social Problems, 41 (3), 383-400.

Based upon 106 in-depth interviews with Black and White police officers and supervisors, from five large municipal agencies in the U.S. Study examines how the social experiences, perspectives, and structural barriers experienced by Black female officers affect their interactions with fellow officers and the general public. The author argues that the combination of race and gender statuses assigned within the station house result in a unique set of problems and perspectives for Black female officers.

Massey, Douglas S., & Nancy A. Denton. (1993). American apartheid: Segregation and the making of the underclass. Cambridge: Harvard University Press.

Using census data from both 1980 and 1990, text explores the degree of residential segregation in the United States. The authors forward the hypothesis that residential segregation is the primary cause of today's Black poor. Reasons for the construction and perpetuation of this structural feature are discussed, as well as the negative social phenomenon often prolific in such communities such as, crime, drugs, and violence.

Mazzella, Ronald, & Alan Feingold. (1994). The effects of physical attractiveness, race, socioeconomic status, and gender of defendants and victims on judgments of mock jurors: A meta-analysis. Journal of Applied Social Psychology, 24 (15), 1315-1344.

Article presents analysis of 80 studies (1969-1994) on the effects of defendant and victim characteristics on mock jurors. Findings reveal that defendants who were physically attractive, female, and had high socio-economic status, received less harsh sanctions than other defendants. Study found no overall race effects. Impact of defendant's race, however, was strongly motivated by crime type. Mock jurors recommended greater punishment for Blacks found guilty of negligent homicide and for Whites found guilty of fraud.

Messerschmidt, James W. (1997). Crime as structured action: Gender, race, class, and crime in the making. Thousand Oaks, CA: Sage.

Author explores relationship between different practices of femininities and masculinities across races and classes to explain the making of crime. Text examines four case studies: lynching during Reconstruction to explore White masculinity; Malcolm X to explore masculinities in hustling and Black power; minority girl gangs to explore the interaction between race, class, and femininity; and the case of the 1986 Challenger explosion, to explore the interaction between class and corporate masculinities among White managers and engineers.

Meyer, Jon'a, & Tara Gray. (1997). Drunk drivers in the courts: Legal and extra-legal factors affecting pleas and sentences. Journal of Criminal Justice, 25 (2),155-163.

Study explores the effects of legal and extra-legal factors on guilty pleas and sentences in drunk driving cases. During a 7-month period in 1993, data were collected from direct observation of arraignments in municipal courtrooms throughout a southern California metropolitan county. Sample includes 200 defendants arraigned for driving under the influence of alcohol. Study indicates that Whites were more than twice as likely to plead not guilty, compared with other racial groups.

Myers, Samuel L., Jr. (1992). Crime, entrepreneurship, and labor force withdrawal. Contemporary Policy Issues, 10 (2), 84-97.

Author explores link between self-reported drug dealing and labor force behavior. Particularly, whether returns to employment influence the decisions by both African-Americans and Whites to enter drug dealing. Analysis is based on the RAND Inmate Survey data collected from male inmates in California, Michigan, and Texas. Findings reveal that Blacks and Whites differ in their perceptions of criminal opportunities. Unattractive labor market opportunities largely explain Black male involvement in drug dealing. Myers argues that current patterns of drug dealing will persist until the labor market raises the legal wages of Blacks to equal that of Whites.

O'Carroll, Patrick, & James Mercy. (1989). Regional variation in homicide rates: Why is the West so violent? Violence and Victims, 4 (1), 17-25.

Study reports the age-adjusted 1980 homicide rates for Whites,

Blacks, and Others for each U.S. state and region. Data were drawn from the National Center for Health Statistics and the U.S. Bureau of the Census. For all racial groups, homicide rates were highest not in the South, but in the West. Homicide rates for Blacks were lower in the South than in any other region of the country. At least for 1980, the high crude homicide rate in the South was the result of two factors: Blacks had a high general homicide rate compared with Whites; and Blacks made up a larger proportion of the Southern population than other regions. It remains unclear whether race-stratified rates of past decades also show this pattern.

Ogawa, Brian K. (1998). Color of justice: Culturally sensitive treatment of minority crime victims. Boston: Allyn and Bacon.

Text explores how victims of crime are handled by nation's justice system. Particularly, the handling of minorities such as Hawaiians, Asian Americans, and Blacks. Author includes personal accounts of the impact of crime on minority communities, hate violence, and media portrayals of crime. Ogawa concludes text with suggestions for redesigning of victim services.

O'Keefe, Maura, & Michal Sela-Amit. (1997). An examination of the effects of race, ethnicity and social class on adolescents' exposure to violence. Journal of Social Service Research, 22 (3), 53-71.

Study explores the influence of race, ethnicity, and social class on adolescents' exposure to violence in their families, schools, and communities. Questionnaire data were obtained from a sample of 899 high school students -- 57 percent Latino, 13 percent Black, 21 percent White, and 8 percent Asian American. Exposure to family violence did not show significant race differences. Race, however, was an important risk factor for exposure to school and community violence. This remained true, even after controlling for social class. Findings support previous research.

Oliver, Mary Beth. (1994). Portrayals of crime, race, and aggression in 'reality-based' police shows: A content analysis. Journal of Broadcasting & Electronic Media, 38 (2), 179-192.

Article presents the findings of a content analysis study completed between 1991-1992. Seventy-six episodes of five "reality-based" police television shows were reviewed to evaluate portrayals of crime, race, and aggression. The findings indicate that these shows tend to overrepresent violent crime, underrepresent Blacks, and overrepresent Whites as police officers. Further, Hispanic and Black suspects were significantly more likely than White suspects to encounter physical aggression by police officers.

Parker, Karen F., & Patricia L. McCall. (1999). Structural conditions and racial homicide patterns: A look at the multiple disadvantages in urban areas. Criminology, 37 (3), 447-478.

Analysis of ways in which structural factors impact homicide rates for Blacks and Whites. Study is based upon 1990 homicide data for U.S. cities with populations of at least 100,000 and at least 2 percent Black. These figures were derived from the U.C.R., census data, and the Comparative Homicide File. Four dependent variables were used: Black Offender/Black Victim homicide rates; White Offender/White Victim homicide rates; Black Offender/White Victim homicide rates; and White Offender/Black Victim homicide rates. Independent variables included local opportunity structure, racial residential segregation, economic deprivation, family disruption, and racial inequality. Findings indicate 1) that improvements in the local opportunity structure are met with a significant reduction in rates of Black intraracial homicide; 2) distinct racial homicide models should be explored; and 3) social isolation for Blacks is substantially greater than for Whites.

Parker, Keith D., Barbara J. McMorris, Earl Smith, & Komanduri S. Murty. (1993). Fear of crime and the likelihood of victimization: A bi-ethnic comparison. Journal of Social Psychology, 133 (5), 723-732.

Article compares fear of crime and the likelihood of future victimization between Hispanics and African Americans, using regression analysis. Analyses based on questionnaires completed by 1,696 Black and 538 Hispanic subway riders from selected sections of New York. Findings reveal that Hispanic respondents are more fearful than Black respondents of being threatened, assaulted, or robbed when riding the subway after dark.

Peeples, Faith, & Rolf Loeber. (1994). Do individual factors and neighborhood context explain ethnic differences in juvenile delinquency? Journal of Quantitative Criminology, 10 (2), 141-157.

Study based upon community sample of 506 White and African American school-age boys living in urban areas. Authors analyze impact of neighborhood and individual factors on juvenile delinquency. Across neighborhoods, African American youths were more likely to be delinquent than White youths. When African American youths did not live in poor areas, however, their rates of delinquency were comparable to White youths. Multiple regression analysis indicates that parental supervision and boys' hyperactivity were the strongest indicators of delinquency.

Peller, Gary. (1993). Criminal law, race, and the ideology of bias: Transcending the critical tools of the sixties. Tulane Law Review, 67 (6), 2231-2252.

Article considers ways in which criminal law interacts with American racism. Peller critiques two assumptions which underlie theorizing on race and the criminal law. First, that significant racial issues involve criminal procedure, not criminal law. Second, that there is an "integrationist" ideology associated with race and criminal law. Peller argues that race-neutral approaches to criminal law are superficial. After rejecting both of these assumptions as ill-informed and problematic, he concludes that an alternative model is preferable. A nationalist approach, which would incorporate alternative views of responsibility, social regulation, and punishment, is offered.

Perry, Ronald W. (1977). Racial discrimination and military justice. New York: Praeger.

Detailed exploration of the impact of race in military criminal proceedings. Focus on treatment of Blacks and Whites in the sea services (navy and marine corps). Research employs multi-variate analysis of Black offending rates and case disposition. Offenses included in analysis: index offenses, status offenses, unauthorized absence, and other military offenses. Author finds little evidence of institutional or systematic discrimination against Blacks.

Petersilia, Joan. (1983). Racial disparities in the criminal justice system. Santa Monica, CA: Rand.

Two-year study evaluates the impact of race on sentencing decisions in California, Michigan, and Texas. Assessment focuses on White, Black, and Hispanic offenders. Data for 1980 was taken from the Offender-Based Transaction Statistics and the RAND Inmate Survey. Findings indicate that race affects two stages of criminal justice processing; post-arrest release and length of sentence. Minorities are more likely to be released following arrest. Once convicted, however, minorities are more likely to receive longer sentences than

Whites.

Pope, Carl E. (1979). Race and crime revisited. Crime and Delinquency, 25 (1), 347-357.

Research evaluates the relationship between crime and race. Focus upon the high rate of Black involvement in the criminal justice system (e.g., arrest, conviction, and incarceration). Author compares self-report data with victim survey studies. It is determined that the differences between official, self-report, and victim survey data pose a methodological dilemma. Further, there is little support for the existence of widespread overt discrimination in the justice system. Future research should consider how system ecology affects decision-making in the criminal justice system.

Reasons, Charles E. (1974). Race, crime and the criminologist. In Charles Reasons (Ed.), The criminologist: Crime and the criminal (pp. 89-97). Pacific Palisades, CA: Goodyear Publishing.

Article offers an overview of the key issues which have influenced criminological thinking on the relationship between race and crime. Specifically, the author considers the dynamic role between societal race relations and ways in which criminologists have evaluated the "racial variable" in criminology. Article also examines the social and political impact of a pursuing race-based crime analysis.

Reasons, Charles E., & Jack L. Kuykendall. (1972). Race, crime, and justice. Pacific Palisades, CA: Goodyear Publishing.

Edited volume addresses the role of race in the application of justice, particularly for Blacks and Native Americans. Topics include: the role of racism in the administration of justice; comparisons of Black and White crime rates; minority community relations with law enforcement; and segregated justice for Native Americans. Text concludes with policy recommendations, such as the further development of police-community relations and the evolution of a more democratic and equitable system of justice.

Rebach, Howard M., Catherine S. Bolek, Katherine L. Williams, & Robert Russell. (1992). Substance abuse among ethnic minorities in America. New York: Garland Press.

Detailed annotated bibliography of research on minorities and drug use. For each entry, authors provide the type of research conducted, purpose of the study, research methods, the results and a critique of the research. Focus is on research about ethnic minorities, including Blacks, Hispanics, American Indians, and Asian and Pacific Islanders. Citations include research published after 1980. Text, which includes more than 150 annotations, also has an author index.

Ross, Luana. (1992). Mothers behind bars: A comparative study of the experiences of imprisoned American Indian and White women (Doctoral dissertation, University of Oregon, 1992). Dissertation Abstracts International, 53 (8), 3002.

Qualitative study which examines experiences of imprisoned American Indian and White mothers gathered from in-depth interviews with twenty-seven incarcerated mothers. The prison warden, treatment specialist, parenting-class facilitator, and social worker were also interviewed. The study explores how experiences and concerns of incarcerated mothers vary by race and examines institutional support enabling imprisoned mothers to maintain family relationships.

Rossi, Peter H., Christine E. Bose, & Richard Berk. (1974). The seriousness of crimes: Normative structure and individual differences. American Sociological Review, 39 (2), 224-237.

Research evaluation of offense seriousness. Survey designed

to assess degree of individual and group consensus on crime seriousness. Baltimore survey participants ranked 140 offenses, ranging from killing a police officer (most serious) to being drunk in a public place (least serious). Analysis included race, sex, age, education, and occupation. Study found agreement across race, sex, and educational level in ordering of crime seriousness.

Ruback, R. Barry, & Paula J. Vardaman. (1997). Decision making in delinquency cases: The role of race and juveniles' admission/denial of the crime. Law and Human Behavior, 21 (1), 47-69.

Article examines the relationship between race and admission of guilt for juveniles. Analysis of archival data from 2,043 adjudication decisions in Georgia found juveniles who admitted guilt were treated more severely than juveniles who denied guilt. Whites were more likely than Blacks to admit committing the crime. After controlling for admission of crime and other legal factors, race was not found to have a significant effect on decision-making. Authors discuss reasons why admission of guilt resulted in more severe punishment.

Ruby, C. L., & John Brigham. (1996). A criminal schema: The role of chronicity, race, and socio-economic status in law enforcement officials' perceptions of others. Journal of Applied Social Psychology, 26 (2), 95-111.

Based upon survey of 120 undergraduate psychology students and 121 police officers, article investigates the extent to which law enforcement officials' perceptions of criminality are biased. Specifically, how their views affected are by race and socio-economic status. Questionnaire focused on perceptions of guilt and other measures of criminality, as well as respondent's demographic background. Analyses revealed that students were more likely to view an ambiguous scenario as criminal than the police officers. When exposed to the actions of a Black or a poor suspect, however, police officers were more likely than students to perceive the suspect as guilty.

Russell, Gregory. (1994). The death penalty and racial bias: Overturning Supreme Court assumptions. Westport, CT: Greenwood Press.

Author tests U.S. Supreme Court's assumption that the procedure used to select jurors who impose the death penalty does not inject racial bias into the jury. Specifically, Russell examines whether the *voir dire* process has a pro-death penalty bias. Data were derived from a Georgia public opinion survey of 917 residents. Findings revealed a consistent but moderate relationship between respondent's race, punitiveness (substitute measure of racial bias), and support for the death penalty. Analysis concludes that "death qualification" tends to eliminate those with moderate attitudes and concentrates racial bias in death penalty juries.

Russell, Katheryn K. (1998). The color of crime: Racial hoaxes, White fear, Black protectionism, police harassment, and other macroaggressions. New York: New York University Press.

Text explores the role race plays in the workings of U.S. criminal justice system. Author provides a historical overview of crime, race, and law, beginning with a discussion of slavery. Russell addresses how racial discrimination is measured in the criminal justice system; 'Driving while Black'; the O.J. Simpson criminal case; how crime is labeled by race (e.g., "Black crime"); and racial hoaxes. Author concludes that more must be done to make the law a more effective tool for redressing racial harms.

Sampson, Robert J., & Janet L. Lauritsen. (1997). Racial and ethnic disparities in crime and criminal justice in the United States. In Michael Tonry (Ed.), Ethnicity, crime, and immigration: Comparative and cross-national perspectives (pp. 311-374).

Chicago: University of Chicago Press.

A detailed overview and assessment of the impact of race and ethnicity in the U.S. criminal justice system. A look at U.C.R. and N.C.V.S. homicide data for Blacks, Whites, and Hispanics. Authors consider theoretical explanations for offending patterns, such as lifestyle-routine activities and subcultural theories. Article also evaluates methodological shortfalls of existing data, including arrest, victimization-based estimates and self-reports. Authors conclude that future race and crime research should include more complex, multi-level analyses; evaluate the cumulative disadvantage across the life course; expand race beyond Whites and Blacks; and consider the impact of crime wars on minority communities.

Sampson, Robert J., & William Julius Wilson. (1995). Toward a theory of race, crime, and urban inequality. In John Hagan and Ruth D. Peterson (Eds.), Crime and inequality (pp.37-54). Stanford, CA: Stanford University Press.

Authors discuss the reluctance of sociologists to confront issues of race and how this has affected the discipline. Sampson and Wilson outline a theoretical strategy which incorporates cultural and structural components. Notably, their model goes beyond economic explanations for criminal involvement. Their community level perspective incorporates factors such as ecological concentration of ghetto poverty, racial segregation, residential mobility, family disruption, and social organization.

Sasson, Theodore, & Margaret K. Nelson. (1996). Danger, community, and the meaning of crime watch: An analysis of the discourses of African American and White participants. Journal of Contemporary Ethnography, 25 (2), 171-200.

Article uses focus group data collected from White and Black residents of Boston, to evaluate the meaning of neighborhood crime watch, by race. While authors found that both Whites and Blacks formed crime watches to improve security and enhance neighborhood solidarity, Black residents were partly motivated by the goal of restoring extended family networks.

Schwartz, Adina. (1996). 'Just take away their guns:' The hidden racism of *Terry v. Ohio*. Fordham Urban Law Journal, XXII (2), 317-375.

A detailed critique of James Q. Wilson's argument that illegal gun use would drop with the increased use of police stops and frisks. Schwartz addresses the proposed impact that such a policy would have on minority motorists, particularly Blacks. Analysis is grounded in a review of U.S. Supreme Court's *Terry v. Ohio* (1968) decision and related case law. Schwartz concludes that though there are insufficient data to indicate the degree to which minorities would be affected by increased police stops, these data are essential before criminologists can propose such policies.

Short, James F., Jr. (1997). Poverty, ethnicity, and violent crime. Boulder, CO: Westview Press.

Relying on statistical trends and ethnographic research on violent crime and gangs, text explores implications surrounding causes of crime for national policy. Author argues violent crime in America is more strongly associated with poverty than race or ethnicity. Further, patterns of violence are changing. Short contends fewer resources should be allocated for prison construction and argues for the redirection of such funds to social policy initiatives within poor communities.

Shusta, Robert M., Deena R. Levine, Phillip R. Harris, & Herb Wong. (1995). Multicultural law enforcement: Strategies for peacekeeping in a diverse society. Englewood Cliffs, NJ: Prentice Hall.

Text focuses on the cross-cultural contact that police officers have with citizens, victims, suspects, and co-workers from diverse backgrounds. Exploration of the pervasive influence of culture, race, and gender in the workplace and in the communities served by law enforcement professionals. Several chapters focus on the interaction between African American, Hispanic, Asian American, and Native American communities and law enforcement.

Simon, David, & Edward Burns. (1997). The corner: A year in the life of an inner-city neighborhood. New York: Broadway Books.

Authors chronicle the corner stories of a poor, inner-city West Baltimore neighborhood. The year-long study captures the lives affected by poverty, drugs, and few economic prospects. Study shows the affect of law enforcement policies, welfare reforms, and "just say no" crusades on inner-city lives. Through DeAndre McCullough's story, authors also paint a picture of a community filled with hope and promise.

Simpson, Sally. S. (1991). Caste, class, and violent crime: Explaining differences in female offending. Criminology, 29 (1), 115-136.

Study examines and explains racial differences in violent female offending. Comparison of violent offending by Black and White females with Black males to demonstrate variance across groups. Article explores potential sources of those differences, specifically relying on three theoretical perspectives to evaluate gender and race differences: neo-Marxism, power-control, and socialist feminist theory. Author concludes that the failure to expand criminology beyond mainstream approaches limits its explanatory power. Consequently, Simpson calls for the expansion of both quantitative and qualitative research on these issues to move the field forward.

Skolnick, Jerome, & James Fyfe. (1993). Above the law: Police
and the excessive use of force. New York: Free Press.

Text explores the use of excessive force by police officers in
the U.S., with particular focus on the 1991 beating of Rodney
King, and discusses the impact of police brutality on public
confidence in law enforcement. Authors outline the causes of
police brutality, including the traditional culture of policing.
Particularly, text assesses how police interpret their role in
current drug enforcement efforts and whether the insularity and
authoritarianism prevalent in some departments may encourage
police brutality. Authors call for administrative reforms,
including the adoption of accountability proceedings against
individual officers which would be monitored by the courts
and general public.

Slansky, David A. (1998). Traffic stops, minority motorists, and the
future of the Fourth Amendment. Supreme Court Review
1997, 271-329.

Article provides a detailed summary and overview of the four
cases decided in the 1996-1997 U.S. Supreme Court term
which address traffic stops involving minority motorists.
These cases are *Whren v. U.S.* (1996), *Ornelas v. U.S.* (1996),
Ohio v. Robinette (1996), and *Maryland v. Wilson* (1997).
After reviewing these decisions, the author concludes that
Supreme Court rulings are problematic given that relief from
racial targeting is neither provided under Fourth Amendment,
nor available elsewhere (e.g., Equal Protection Clause).

Smith, Carolyn, & Marvin Krohn. (1995). Delinquency and
family life among male adolescents: The role of ethnicity.
Journal of Youth and Adolescents, 24 (1), 69-93.

Study examines the role of ethnic and racial diversity in the
relationship between family processes and delinquency. Based
upon data from two waves of the Rochester (N.Y.) Youth

Development Study in which face-to-face interviews of seventh and eighth grade males were conducted in 1987-1988, authors find that family variables as a group are more important in constraining delinquency for Hispanics than for African Americans and Whites.

Spohn, Cassia C. (1990). The sentencing decision of Black and White judges: Expected and unexpected similarities. Law and Society, 24 (5), 1197-1214.

A test of the hypothesis that White judges and Black judges reach different sentencing conclusions in criminal cases. Study includes sample of 13 Black and 25 White judges from Detroit Recorder's Court and 8,414 Black and White offenders tried in this court, between 1976 and 1979. Findings indicate that race of judge offers little predictive power for sentencing outcomes. Black and White judges reached similar sentencing decisions and both sentenced Black offenders more harshly than White offenders.

Spohn, Cassia C. (1995). Courts, sentences, and prisons. Daedalus, 124 (1), 119-143.

Essay examines the current Southern criminal justice system in light of the reforms proposed by Gunnar Myrdal in An American Dilemma. Author contends that while such reforms have all but eliminated overt racist behaviors directed against Black defendants, they have yet to produce equality of justice. Spohn notes that discrimination persists in all stages of the criminal justice system. Discussion focuses on recent findings concerning the relationship between race and sexual assault cases and the imposition of the death penalty.

Spohn, Cassia C., & Jerry Cederblom. (1991). Race and disparities in sentencing: A test of the liberation hypothesis. Justice Quarterly, 8 (3), 305-327.

Test of Harry Kalven and Hans Zeisel's liberation hypothesis which maintains that in cases with weak or contradictory evidence, jurors are more likely to consider extra legal variables, such as race. Authors examine whether racial discrimination in sentencing is more likely in low-level cases. Study based upon 4,655 cases involving Black and White offenders tried in Detroit Recorder's Court between 1976 and 1979. Multiple regression analysis indicates that the sentencing decision reflects both direct and indirect racial discrimination. Findings, which support liberation hypothesis, show a significant race effect in less serious cases.

Staples, Robert. (1975, March). White racism, Black crime, and American justice: An application of the colonial model to explain crime and race. Pyhlon, 36, 14-22.

Article offers a "colonial" model to explain the relationship between race and crime. This theoretical model, based on the work of Frantz Fanon, treats the Black community as an underdeveloped colony. This colony, controlled by Whites, is subject to harsher standards of justice than other communities. The colonial model predicts that crimes committed within Black communities are more likely to be punished and more likely to elicit harsher sanctions. Staples outlines the treatment of interracial crimes (e.g., Black-on-White) under the colonial model and how the agents of the state (e.g., police) interact with colonized groups.

Steffensmeier, Darrell, Jeffrey Ulmer, & John Kramer. (1998). The interaction of race, gender and age in criminal sentencing: The punishment cost of being young, Black, and male. Criminology, 36 (4), 763-798.

Authors evaluate impact of "focal concerns" on judicial decision-making. Specifically, article explores the role of offender blameworthiness and victim harm, protection of community, and the practical affect of sentencing decisions.

Pennsylvania sentencing outcomes from 1989 to 1992 are used. Authors find that race is more likely to impact the sentencing of young men and that Black men receive harshest sentences. Further, age is more likely to impact sentencing of men. Empirical findings support use of interactive over additive sentencing models.

Stokes, Larry D., & James F. Scott. (1996). Affirmative action and selected minority groups in law enforcement. Journal of Criminal Justice, 24 (1), 29-38.

Using data obtained from police chiefs and public safety commissioners in 19 municipal police departments, article explores political controversy surrounding use of affirmative action and race-norming in law enforcement. Also examines minority representation in each of the 19 departments, specifically, the presence of Hispanic, Asian, and female officers. Findings indicate that Hispanic representation most closely matched overall Hispanic representation in society. In absolute numbers, females were the most populous of the three groups. Article concludes with a discussion of whether culturally diverse police forces improve agency effectiveness in the community.

Tonry, Michael. (1995). Malign neglect: Race, crime, and punishment in America. New York: Oxford University Press.

Text examines how crime and social policy has evolved and their impact on Black communities. Author reviews the involvement of Blacks and Whites in the criminal justice system, including a look at arrest, sentencing and incarceration rates. Tonry critiques the War on Drugs and its deleterious impact on communities of color. He concludes text with proposals for sound social and racial policies, including an assessment of the racial impact of proposed policies, and individualized justice.

Townsend, Tara Noelle. (1996). Is justice color blind? The effect of race on perceptions of crime severity (Doctoral dissertation, Temple University, 1996). Dissertation Abstracts International, 57 (6), 4095.

Study addresses racial discrimination from an individual, rather than institutional perspective. Specifically, author examines the effect of race on individual perceptions of crime severity. Analysis, based on simulated jury study that employed a full factorial design, reveals that race is a prominent variable used to evaluate criminal incidents. The total influence of race on decision-making, however, is not always predictable.

Tuch, Steven A., & Ronald Weitzer. (1997). Racial differences in attitudes toward the police. Public Opinion Quarterly Volume, 61 (4), 642-663.

Article presents findings of time-series analysis based on three polls, the National Opinion Research Center, Gallup Poll, and a *The Los Angeles Times* poll. Analysis focuses on three questions: whether publicized incidents of brutality alter public attitudes toward the police; whether African-Americans, Latinos, and Whites have different reactions; and whether incidents remain part of the public psyche ("staying power"). Research centers on polls taken before and after three high-profile police brutality cases, including the 1979 killing of Eula Love, the 1991 beating of Rodney King, and the 1996 police beating of two Mexican immigrants. Findings show that public support for the police declines following a publicized incident of brutality. Blacks show greatest decline in support, followed by Latinos, then Whites. Incidents of police brutality have greatest staying power for Blacks and Latinos, followed by Whites.

Tucker, William H. (1994). The science and politics of racial research. Chicago: University of Illinois Press.

Incisive examination of how research on race has evolved. Author provides a detailed analysis of the perspectives and approaches to race by 19th and 20th century researchers. Text indicates the breadth of researcher bias in formulating, testing, and explaining "scientific" findings on race. Tucker highlights and explores the politics and racism behind eugenics movement and contemporary examples of this ideology.

Valdez, Avelardo, Zenong Yin, & Charles Kaplan. (1997). A comparison of alcohol, drugs, and aggressive crime among Mexican-American, Black, and White male arrestees in Texas. American Journal of Drug and Alcohol Abuse, 23 (2), 249-265.

Article examines relationship between aggressive behavior and substance abuse in Mexican-American, Black, and White males. Drawing on 1992 interview and drug test data of 2,364 male arrestees in Houston, Dallas, and San Antonio, authors found Mexican-Americans were most likely to be arrested for aggressive crimes. For all ethnic groups, drug users and heavy drinkers were less likely to be charged with aggressive crimes than those who drank or used drugs infrequently. Authors suggest additional research is needed to examine the correlation between substance abuse and aggression across ethnic groups, as well as varying social contexts.

Walker, Samuel, & Molly A. Brown. (1995). Pale reflection of reality: The neglect of racial and ethnic minorities in introductory criminal justice textbooks. Journal of Criminal Justice Education, 6 (1), 61-83.

Employing both quantitative and qualitative methods, article examines how issues of race and ethnicity are covered in 13 contemporary introductory criminal justice textbooks, published between 1990 and 1994. Each of the texts failed to cover core issues related to race and ethnicity, such as: arrest, police use of force, charging and plea bargaining, sentencing, and the death penalty. Instead, volumes presented a mechanistic approach to the administration of justice, limited focus to Black Americans, and mistakenly relied upon celebrated cases in their portrayal of the American criminal justice system.

Walker, Samuel, Cassia C. Spohn, & Miriam DeLone. (1995). The color of justice: Race, ethnicity, and crime in America. Belmont, CA: Wadsworth.

Text offers wide-ranging exploration of the impact race has upon criminal justice system participants. Specifically, offender and victim issues are discussed and analyzed. Volume addresses race and policing, arrest, prosecutorial charging, jury selection, sentencing, incarceration, and capital punishment. Walker and colleagues consider other variables which intersect with race to affect criminal justice system outcomes (e.g., socio-economic status) and provide a historical back-drop for discussions.

Weitzer, Ronald. (1996). Racial discrimination in the criminal justice system: Findings and problems in the literature. Journal of Criminal Justice, 24 (4), 309-322.

Race-based conflict theory predicts substantial, institutionalized discrimination against minorities within criminal justice systems. This article examines the nature and extent of racial discrimination by police, courts, and correctional agencies in the United States. The body of research analyzed points to racial effects at certain points in the criminal justice system and in certain contexts. Further, author concludes that discrimination is less extensive than conflict theory predicts.

Williams, Terry. (1989). Cocaine kids. Reading, MA: Addison-Wesley.

Ethnographic study of teenagers engaged in crack-cocaine trade. Based on research gathered by sociologist who chronicled four-year period of low-level drug dealing. From 1983-1986, researcher engaged in participant-observation with Black and Hispanic New York youths. Work details the lives of the youths, socio-economic context of their drug-selling and the consequences of their involvement in crime.

Willie, Charles V., & Ozzie Edwards. (1983). Race and crime. In Sanford Kadish (Ed.), Encyclopedia of crime and justice, Vol. 4 (pp.1347-1350). New York: The Free Press.

Entry provides brief summary of research on crime and race. Authors also include overview of social science explanations of the role race plays in causing crime. Particular focus on disproportionate offending by minorities. Entry provides overview of the impact of socio-economic status, acting-out behavior, civil disorder, and communties on criminal offending.

Wolfgang, Marvin E., & Bernard Cohen. (1970). Crime and race: Conceptions and misconceptions. New York: Institute of Human Relations Press.

Report addresses causes and extent of crime among African Americans. While numerous biological explanations have been forwarded, particularly by White criminologists, the authors argue that there is no empirical evidence that lends credence to any genetic theory of crime. Rather, Wolfgang and Cohen note that greater support is found in environmental explanations. Specifically, the majority of Blacks live in an environment characterized by substandard education, housing, and employment conditions. Until discrimination is eliminated and more educational and vocational resources are provided, the authors contend that Blacks will be unable to compete with Whites in the socio-economic arena.

Wolfgang, Marvin, & Marc Riedel. (1973, May). Race, judicial discretion and the death penalty. Annals of the American Academy of Political and Social Science, 407, 119-133.

Authors contend that racial differentials in the use of the death penalty may not alone reveal the existence of racial discrimination. The *Furman v. Georgia* (1972) decision is discussed. Authors review some earlier studies of racial differentials in sentencing and summarize research procedures and conclusions from an elaborate study of sentencing for rape in states where that offense has been a capital crime. When non-racial aggravating situations are considered, there is strong statistical significant differences in proportions of Blacks sentenced to death, compared with Whites.

Young, Vernetta D. (1980). Women, race, and crime. Criminology, 18 (1), 26-34.

Exploration of Freda Adler's (1975) posited relationships between sex, race, and crime. Specifically, that Black female offending more closes matches Black male offending than White female offending matches White male offending. Further, that there is a larger gap between Black/White female offending than Black/White male offending. National Crime Survey data for 1972-1975 are used to test these hypotheses. Findings fail to support Adler's proposed relationships. Young concludes that future research should include official data and include a broader range of crimes (e.g., white-collar offending).

Zatz, Marjorie S. (1984). Race, ethnicity, and determinate sentencing: A new dimension to an old controversy. Criminology, 22 (2), 147-171.

Article presents the findings from a California study on sentencing. Research evaluates the impact of race on sentencing outcomes for Whites, Blacks, and Chicanos. Study found race had an indirect effect on sentencing. Specifically, offense type, case disposition, and prior record influence the sentencing decision. Findings support the need to examine sentencing patterns for Chicanos separately from other racial groups.

Zatz, Marjorie S. (1987). The changing forms of racial/ethnic biases in sentencing. Journal of Research in Crime and Delinquency, 24 (1), 69-92.

Article provides an overview of the research on racial discrimination in the criminal justice system, from the 1930s to the 1980s. Research is divided into four historical "waves." Author focuses on how research was conducted during each of these intervals, with particular attention given to research methods, data sources, sociological context in which research was conducted, and forms of racial bias within the justice system. Article also discusses impact of determinate sentencing laws.

Part 7

Special Issues, Edited Volumes, and Guides

Bedau, Hugo (Ed.). (1997). The death penalty in America: Current controversies. New York: Oxford University Press.

Essays by authors on both sides of the capital punishment debate. Anthology draws from a wide range of perspectives to present a comprehensive view of death penalty issues. Select essays address the constitutionality of death penalty legislation and its application, the controversy surrounding support for the death penalty, the debate between capital punishment and life imprisonment, and the affect of race and class.

Blacks and crime - Can America break the chain of failure? [Special Issue]. (1978). Nation's Cities, 16 (9).

Article utilizes quantitative data on index offenses, victims, and criminal justice personnel to challenge commonly-held negative views concerning Blacks and crime. Authors argue that contrary to popular opinion, race is not a major factor in either victimization or crime. Rather, factors such as residence, age, and gender are stronger predictors. Additionally, authors find that crime and fear of crime in lower socio-economic communities contribute to such patterns through the creation of feelings of isolation, withdrawal and aggressiveness. Contributors include: Lee Brown, William

Drake, John Warren, and Hubert Williams.

Bridges, George S., & Martha A. Myers (Eds.). (1994). Inequality, crime, and social control. Boulder, CO: Westview Press.

Focus on inequality, crime, and social control in society. Text addresses several topics, such as whether sociologists can reconcile conflicting theoretical perspectives on crime and whether inequality research should be expanded to include a larger group of subjugated persons. Proposals for future research are included.

Developments in the law: Race and the criminal process. (1988). Harvard Law Review, 101 (7), 1472-1641.

Comprehensive overview of legal and empirical research on race and crime. Volume explores the impact of race on constitutional protections, including equal protection and due process. This review provides a detailed discussion of the impact of race and police abuse, prosecutorial discretion, jury selection, juror misconduct, capital punishment, and sentencing.

Finkelman, Paul. (1993). Symposium on the law of slavery. [Special Issue]. Chicago-Kent Law Review, 68 (3).

Seventeen articles address the wide-ranging conditions of U.S. chattel slavery. Works explore the institution of slavery, such as treatment of slaves, rape of slave women, and the impact of slavery on slaves and slaveholders. Articles also examine philosophical questions posed by slavery, including whether it was morally justifiable. Several articles include legal analysis of criminal trials involving slaves. Contributors include Derrick Bell, Thomas Morris, and Judith Schafer.

Fraser, Steven (Ed.). (1995). The bell curve wars: Race, intelligence, and the future of America. New York: Basic

Books.

Text critiques arguments made in The Bell Curve. Twenty essays address wide-ranging issues, including empirical methods, timing of the publication, history of racial research, and meritocracy. Contributors include Henry Louis Gates, Jr., Stephen Jay Gould, Andrew Hacker, Randall Kennedy, and Thomas Sowell.

Gary, Lawrence E., & Lee P. Brown (Eds). (1975). Crime and its impact on the Black community. Washington, DC: Institute for Urban Affairs and Research.

Edited volume includes writings by academics, journalists, and criminal justice system professionals. Eighteen essays explore range of topics including the historical treatment of Blacks and crime; definitions of crime; media images; Black perspectives on crime; and policing in the Black community. Contributors include Lee Brown, Lenwood Davis, Charles Owens, Elsie Scott, and Robert Staples.

Georges-Abeyie, Daniel. (Ed.). (1984). The criminal justice system and Blacks. New York: Clark Boardman Company.

Edited volume of 20 original and reprinted articles, as well as executive summaries. Addresses the relationship between race, crime, justice, and victimization. Text is divided into three parts: The first part examines the impact of racial/ethnic definitions on crime and victimization research; part two addresses the treatment of Blacks and other minorities by various criminal justice agencies; and part three focuses on causes and consequences of current incarceration rates for African Americans, as well as presents a number of policy recommendations. Volume concludes with an interview with retired judge Bruce Wright.

Harrell, Adele V., & George E. Peterson (Eds.). (1992). Drugs,

crime, and social isolation: Barriers to urban opportunity.
Washington, DC: Urban Institute Press.

Collection of nine essays examines the isolation of the U.S.
inner city and the subsequent impact on its residents. In
particular, a number of ethnographic studies explore the impact
of physical and social isolation on crime in urban centers.
New York, Philadelphia, and Chicago are among the cities
included in these studies.

Hawkins, Darnell F. (Ed.). (1995). Ethnicity, race, and crime:
Perspectives across time and place. Albany, NY: State
University of New York Press.

Edited volume examines issues of crime and various racial and
ethnic groups, including Hispanics, Native Americans, Asian
Americans, Blacks, and Whites. Articles offer contemporary
analyses as well as assessments of justice system processing.
Further, text provides mix of theoretical and empirical
analyses. Policing, drugs, and lynching are among the topic
areas covered. Articles written by researchers of various race
and ethnic backgrounds. Contributors include E. M. Beck,
Robert Crutchfield, Gary LaFree, Coramae Richey Mann, Joan
McCord, Martha Myers, and Stewart Tolnay.

Hendricks, James E., & Bryan Byers (Eds.). (1994). Multicultural
perspectives in criminal justice and criminology. Springfield,
IL: U.S.A.

Compilation of articles addresses issues related to the
multicultural nature of the United States criminal justice
system. Text examines both the adult and juvenile offending
populations. Text is an anthology of 12 essays and reviews on
multicultural perspectives in criminology and criminal justice.
Contributors include Steven Chermak, Laura Myers, Dennis
Rome, and Lori Spillane.

Horn, C., & Curt T. Griffiths. (1989). Native North Americans: Crime, conflict and criminal justice bibliography. Burnaby, BC: Simon Fraser University Press.

Special bibliography provides catalogue of research, policy and programs involving American Indians and the criminal justice systems in the United States, Canada, and Greenland. Specific topics include: health and welfare; education; drug abuse,; constitutional rights and jurisdictional issues; tribal justice systems; and crime patterns.

Huff, C. Ronald (Ed.). (1996). Gangs in America. Thousand Oaks, CA: Sage.

Volume brings together a collection of papers on gangs. Provides an assessment of behavioral, ecological and socio-economic dimensions of gangs. Includes a discussion of the role of ethnicity and gender. Particularly, how the decline in White gangs, except in smaller cities, has resulted in predominantly Hispanic and African American gangs. Text also includes analysis of the emergence of gangs from several Asian countries in several U.S. cities.

Indian tribal courts and justice: A symposium [Special issue]. (1995). Judicature, 79 (3).

Anthology presents viewpoints of professionals who have direct contact with and knowledge of the intricacy of the indigenous justice system. Discussion of the federal, state, and tribal court systems. Topics include: federal commitment to tribal justice system; development of tribal courts from past to present; issues surrounding jurisdictional dilemmas; and role of tribal courts in an indigenous society.

Jacoby, Russell, & Naomi Glauberman (Eds.). (1995). The bell curve debate: History, documents, opinions. New York: Times Books.

140 Race and Crime

Text presents collection of articles, essays, and other materials which address issues raised by The Bell Curve. Editors include historical documents on race, racism, and science; writings and interviews by those who support and oppose conclusions reached in The Bell Curve; and material written after the publication of Herrnstein and Murray's book. Text explores wide range of issues, including merits of intelligence testing, athleticism and race, ethics of eugenics, race and the scientific method, and distinctions between race and ethnicity.

Joshi, S.T. (1999). Documents of American prejudice: An anthology of writings on race from Thomas Jefferson to David Duke. New York: Basic Books.

Compilation of vast array of historical and contemporary documents related to race. These include writings by presidents, historians, journalists, social scientists, biologists, politicians, and supreme court justices. A number of the writings offer and refute the use of race as a basis for discriminatory treatment. Volume divided into various topic areas, including science and pseudo science; Aryans, Anglo-Saxons and Teutons; Manifest Destiny and imperialism; social Darwinism and eugenics; prejudice and religion; Native Americans, African Americans, Jews, Asian Americans, Latinos; and immigration.

Kedia, P. Ray (Ed.). (1994). Black on Black crime: Facing facts--challenging fictions. Bristol, IN: Wyndham Hall Press.

Anthology of 10 essays and studies which examine Black-on-Black crime in the United States. The contributors tackle various topics, including the influence of Eurocentric interpretations of Black violence, the historical factors which explain White fear of victimization by Blacks, and the impact of the media's emphasis on Black on Black crime.

Latinos and the criminal justice system: A view from both sides of the bar [Special issue]. (1994). Harvard Latino Law Review, 1 (1).

Includes five essays and book reviews. Articles address Hispanic involvement in criminal justice processing, including the disproportionate representation of Hispanics and the impact of courtroom language interpreters. Also includes a look at the Federal Sentencing Guidelines and gang violence.

Leonard, Kimberly Kempf, Carl E. Pope, & William H. Feyerherm (Eds.). (1995). Minorities in juvenile justice. Thousand Oaks, CA: Sage.

Text is a collection of research and policy papers that address the extent and sources of disparate treatment of minority youth, including African Americans, Asian Americans, Latinos, and Native Americans within the juvenile justice system. Papers respond to 1988 Congressional amendment to Juvenile Justice and Delinquency Prevention Act. This amendment requires states to investigate overrepresentation of minority youths in confinement. Goal of compilation is to provide cumulative look at juvenile confinement and states' responses to the problem.

Lopez, Antoinette Sedillo (Ed.). (1995). Latinos in the United States: History, law and perspective. New York: Garland.

Anthology of 15 previously unpublished articles (written since 1980) which explore the impact of criminal justice system reform on the Latino community. Articles include Tobias Duran's exploration of how the law impacts power relationships between Hispanics and Whites; Hisauro Garza's look at the administration of justice for Chicanos; David Carter's discussion of Hispanic perceptions of police performance in Texas; and Alfredo Mirande's analyses of community-police conflict and fear of crime in a Chicano community.

Lynch, Michael J., & E. Britt Patterson (Eds.). (1991). Race and criminal justice. Albany, NY: Harrow and Heston.

Volume explores both the formal and informal biases minorities encounter at various stages of the criminal justice system. Treatment of both adult and juvenile offenders is examined. Volume covers several crime and race issues. Topics include treatment of immigrants within the criminal justice system, capital punishment, ethnic bias in corrections, racially-motivated crimes, and Black overrepresentation in the juvenile justice system. Contributors include Frankie Bailey, Robert Bohm, Billy Close, Carol Lujan, Zoann Snyder-Joy, and Ted Tollett.

Lynch, Michael J., & E. Britt Patterson (Eds.). (1996). Justice with prejudice: Race and criminal justice in America. Albany, NY: Harrow and Heston.

Text is editors' follow-up to an earlier volume (Race and Criminal Justice, 1991). This compilation examines theoretical, qualitative, and empirical assessments of racial bias in U.S. criminal justice system. Topic areas include: family structure and its impact on crime; role media plays in the creation and perpetuation of racial bias in criminal stereotypes; and the interrelated roles of racism, stereotypes, politics, and academia in the criminal justice system. Contributors include Theodore Chiricos, Charles Corley, Jacklyn Huey, and Mahesh Nalla.

MacLean, Brian D. & Dragan Milovanovic (Eds.). (1990). Racism, empiricism and criminal justice. Vancouver, Canada: Collective Press.

Anthology of 17 essays arranged around a discussion of the prevalence of discrimination against minorities in the justice system. First section critiques William Wilbanks' "no discrimination" hypothesis on substantive and methodological grounds. Second section broadens the critique to examine its applicability to minority relations in jurisdictions outside the United States. Text concludes with select authors evaluating the arguments. Contributors include Daniel Georges-Abeyie, Michael Lynch, Coramae Richey Mann, William Wilbanks, and Marjorie Zatz.

Mann, Coramae Richey, & Marjorie Zatz (Eds.). (1998). Images of color, images of crime: Readings. Belmont, CA: Wadsworth.

A comprehensive examination of racial and ethnic discrimination in America's criminal justice system. Text provides an investigative overview of patterns of criminal behavior, victimization, and life experiences of minority populations in the United States. Essays explore crime, criminal justice, and media images of Latinos, Blacks, Asians and Native Americans. Essays also consider White criminality. Volume includes more than 20 contributors.

Martinez, Ramiro F., Jr., & Valerie P. Hans (Eds.). (1994). Race, ethnicity, and the law [Special issue]. Law and Human Behavior, 18 (3).

Volume explores law, race, and ethnicity. Issue covers theoretical and empirical analyses. Most articles address criminal justice issues, including racial prejudice in the Canadian legal system; the racial inequality hypothesis; racial mistrust and deviance among Caribbean adolescents; and capital punishment. Contributors include Robert Bohm, Katheryn Russell, and Dorothy Taylor. Afterword by Darnell Hawkins.

McCord, Joan (Ed.). (1997). Violence and childhood in the inner city. Cambridge, MA: Cambridge Univeristy Press.

Text addresses various ways that violence impacts minority juveniles in urban settings. Authors explore macro-level

influences on youth violence through an analysis of historical
and contemporary factors. Micro-level causes, such as
psychology and biology, are also considered. Topics cover
community-level perspectives on violence, inner-city street
codes, neuropsychology, and child abuse. Contributors include
Elijah Anderson, Felton Earls, Terrie Moffitt, and Robert
Sampson.

Myers, Samuel L., Jr., & Margaret C. Simms. (1988). The
economics of race and crime. New Brunswick, NJ:
Transaction Books.

Eleven articles on race and crime. Text divided into two parts.
First section includes landmark articles by early race and crime
scholars, such as W.E.B. Du Bois, Thorsten Sellin, W.F.
Willcox, and Monroe Work. These articles explore structural
and individual reasons for the high Black crime rate. The
second part includes frontier articles which emphasize
quantitative analysis. Authors include Richard Freeman and
William Sabol. These articles address the relationship
between employment and criminality for Black and White
youths.

Nordquist, Joan. (1997). Race, crime and the criminal justice
system: A bibliography. Santa Cruz, CA: Reference and
Research Services.

Bibliography includes books, book chapters, journal articles,
government documents, and dissertations on race, ethnicity,
and the criminal justice system in the United States. Citations
to material on African Americans, Latinos, Asian Americans,
and Native Americans. Topic areas include: race, ethnicity,
and the criminal justice system; and race, ethnicity, inequality,
and criminality.

Owens, Charles E., & Jimmy Bell (Eds.). (1977). Blacks and criminal
justice. Lexington, MA: Lexington Books.

Thirteen authors contribute to this volume which explores issues relating to Blacks in the U.S. criminal justice system. These essays address a wide range of issues relating to Black involvement in the justice system. Topics include victimization, prison education, police-community relations, and the impact of socio-economic factors on incarceration. Authors include researchers, practitioners, and community organizers.

Pope, Carl, & Todd Clear (Eds.). (1994). Race and punishment [Special issue]. Journal of Research in Crime and Delinquency, 31 (2).

Special issue devoted to race, punishment, and the criminal justice system. Articles address theoretical issues, and qualitative and quantitative research methods. Articles explore impact of race in juvenile detention decisions, capital punishment, perceived sanction threats, and sentencing disparity. Authors include Brenda Sims Blackwell, Darlene Conley, Robert Crutchfield, and Madeline Wordes.

Reynolds, Gerald A. (Ed.). (1996). Race and the criminal justice system: How race affects jury trials. Washington, DC: Center for Equal Opportunity.

Compilation of 12 essays which examine the impact of race on jury trials in the United States. Some findings are based on quantitative data analyses, other analyses are anecdotal. Topics areas include: the history of racially-based jury verdicts in the U.S.; cases involving a hung jury or acquittal by minority jurors of a minority defendant, despite significant evidence of guilt; an examination of whether a juror's education and economic status are better predictors of verdicts than race; and the debate surrounding the use of racial quotas in jury selection and composition.

Rosen, Lawrence. (1976). American Indians and the law.

Piscataway, NJ: Distribution Transaction Publishers Rutgers-the State University.

Symposium of nine articles addresses range of issues surrounding Indian law. Text begins with a discussion of the unique position of American Indians within the United States society and the special legal status they are assigned under federal policies. Particular attention is directed to the historical development and purpose of the Bureau of Indian Affairs, as well as select federal legislation that have a direct impact on indigenous populations.

Ross, Lee E. (1998). African American criminologists, 1970-1996: An annotated bibliography. Westport, CT: Greenwood Press.

Annotations of articles, books, and dissertations written by African American criminologists from 1970 to 1996. Editor observes that despite the accomplishments of these criminologists, they have been largely overlooked in criminal justice curricula and policy. Reference guide compiled to make the work of Black criminologists more accessible.

Schwartz, Martin, & Dragan Milovanovic (Eds.). (1996). Race, gender and class in criminology: The intersection. Chicago: Third World Press.

A collection of essays drawn from conflict, feminist, left realism, postmodern, and peacemaking theoretical perspectives. Text examines how issues of race, gender, and class have been treated within criminology. Divided into two sections, essays first address the relationship of these three factors in a broad theoretical context, then the focus is on specific applications. Topics include: sentencing adult female offenders to prison, the intersection of race, class, and gender issues in white-collar crime and decision making in the juvenile system as it applies to female juvenile offenders.

Sherman, Francine T., & William Talley, Jr. (Eds.). (1995). Symposium--struggling for a future: Juvenile violence, juvenile justice [Special issue]. Boston College Law Review, 36 (5).

Issue features six papers from 1994 conference on juvenile violence and justice. Essays discuss: responsibility of African-American community to address current rates of violence in inner-cities, in addition to seeking federal aid when developing strategies to combat violence, racism, and sexism; abolition of existing structures of juvenile and adult criminal justice systems in favor of a unified system that focuses on individual characteristics of the defendant; the expansion of juvenile system to incorporate same due process protections found in adult system; enhancement of juvenile court authority to order extended dispositions in serious cases; and theoretical explanations for current construction of juvenile system.

Stalans, Loretta J., & Arthur J. Lurigio (Eds.). (1996). Public opinion on justice in the criminal justice system [Special issue]. American Behavioral Scientist, 39 (4).

Ten studies and reviews of public opinion in the United States about the criminal justice system. Special issue addresses such topics as: the role of the media on the general public's perception and fear of crime; racial differences in the endorsement of deadly force by police officers; the level of public support for mandatory sentencing practices (e.g., three strikes statutes); and the rationale behind public support for the death penalty. Both qualitative and quantitative data are discussed.

Standing Bear, Z. G., & Richard C. Monk (Eds.). (1992). Race, crime, and criminal justice [Special Issue]. Journal of Contemporary Criminal Justice, 8 (2).

Special issue focusing on race and crime. Articles cover topics including homicide rates and race; analysis of race and ethnicity; philosophy and representations of race; and the Canadian criminal justice system. Contributors include Jay Corzine, Daniel Georges-Abeyie, Alexander Hooke, Lin Huff-Corzine, Allan Patenaude, and M. Dwayne Smith.

Sulton, Ann Thomas (Ed.). (1994). African-American perspectives on: Crime causation, criminal justice administration and crime prevention. Englewood, CO: Sulton Books.

Edited volume features articles written by African-American criminologists and criminal justice practitioners. Text focuses on urban crime, including youth violence, gangs, drugs, victimization of foreigners, police brutality, and A.I.D.S. in correctional facilities. Further, several authors make policy recommendations for urban crime control and prevention. Contributors include Laura Fishman, Sampson Oli, Lee Ross, Elsie Scott, Charles See, Becky Tatum, Dorothy Taylor, Helen Taylor-Greene, and Vernetta Young.

Symposium: Minority Scholarship in Crime and Justice. (1992). Justice Quarterly, 9 (4).

Collection of nine articles written by Asian and African American criminologists. Topic areas include Asian gangs, relationship between self-esteem and delinquency, impact of race on criminal justice ideology, development of a Black criminology, and attitudes of Chinese and Vietnamese immigrants toward police. Contributors include Roy Austin, Sandra Browning, Liqun Cao, Ko-Lin Chin, Charisse Coston, Willie Edwards, Lee Ross, Katheryn Russell, John Huey-Long Song, and Calvin Toy.

Symposium on Race and Criminal Justice. (1994). Washington and Lee Law Review, 51 (2).

Volume explores the effect of race on the everyday operations of the criminal justice system. Focus is on treatment of Blacks in the justice system. Symposium includes four articles and four essays. Topics include racial discrimination in the application of the death penalty; ways in which the justice system operates as a dragnet for Black men; and an empirical assessment of how race, racism, and race issues are handled in the courtroom. Contributors include David Baldus, Kathleen Daly, Coramae Richey Mann, Jerome Miller, and Bryan Stevenson.

Trostle, Lawrence C. (Ed.). (1994). Rural justice [Special issue]. Journal of Contemporary Criminal Justice, 10 (2).

Special issue focuses on the delivery of criminal justice services to remote jurisdictions in the United States. Focus on indigenous populations found in Northern Alaska. Topics include: historical overview of U.S. efforts at policing American Indian populations, and the jurisdictional issues that arise from such policies and practices; theoretical explanations of current efforts at policing indigenous tribes of Northern Alaska; overview of justice system in rural Alaska, focusing on delivery of services to small, isolated villages; and policy analysis that explores the melding of traditional Native and Western values in Alaskan state courts, as well as village tribal courts.

Wang, Zheng (Ed.). (1996). Organized crime V: Asian gangs. Part I [Special issue]. Journal of Contemporary Criminal Justice, 12 (4).

Features five articles on Asian gangs and organized crime groups in the United States. Topics include the evolution of Vietnamese crime groups, the presence of Chinese gangs and organized crime groups in Chicago, the development of Laotian street gangs in Dallas, and the structure and migration patterns of Hong Kong based triad groups. Wide-ranging articles include analyses of trend data, qualitative research methods, reviews of international issues, and considerations of political implications of Asian crime.

Ware, Gilbert (Ed.). (1976). From the Black bar - Voices for equal justice. New York: Putnam.

Anthology compiled by Black authorities in the criminal justice system. Essays address role of racism in the application of justice, constitutional rights, and civil liberties of African Americans, prisoners' rights, and school desegregation. Contributors include African American attorneys and judges, and Justice Thurgood Marshall.

Part 8

Government Documents, Reports, and Commission Findings

Advisory Board's Report to the President. President's Initiative on Race. (1998). One America in the 21st century: Forging a new future. Washington, D.C.: U.S. Government Printing Office.

Comprehensive report on U.S. race relations at end of 20th century. Report is based upon a national review by seven-member Presidential panel, headed by historian John Hope Franklin. Report includes discussion of various racial and ethnic groups, including Asian Americans, Whites, Hispanics, American Indians, and Blacks. Explores majority group versus minority group tensions as well as conflicts between people of color. Study addresses wide range of social issues such as education, poverty, health, welfare, and housing. Media representations of race are also considered. Report concludes with "ten things that every American should do."

American Bar Association. (1994). Achieving justice in a diverse America: Summit on racial and ethnic bias in the justice system. Chicago: Author.

Compilation of essays presented at A.B.A. summit on racial and ethnic bias in the U.S. criminal justice system. Text contains background on Native American, Hispanic National, and National Asian Pacific Bar Associations, and presents reforms recommended by the A.B.A. Task Force on Minorities and the Justice System both the criminal and civil systems should adopt in their treatment of minority defendants. Specific focus is directed to barriers to racial and ethnic justice, death penalty issues, strategies to increase minority recruitment and retention in criminal justice administration, and proposals to increase system's ability to mete out justice.

American Bar Association. (1999). Race and the law [Special Issue]. A.B.A. Journal, 85.

Special report on race and the law, which explores viewpoints on race held by Black and White lawyers. Study indicates there are racially-divergent opinions. For example, 98 percent of Black lawyers believe there is "very much" or "some" racial bias in the justice system, compared with 62 percent for Whites. Journal addresses lawyers' perspectives on impact of race upon jury selection, law firm partnership selection, federal clerkship selection, judicial nominations, and racial profiling.

American Correctional Association. (1993). Gangs in correctional facilities: A national assessment. Lanham, MD: Author.

Overview of gang activity in U.S. correctional facilities. Report draws upon survey data from 98 federal, state, and local correctional systems. Research indicates that there are at least four identifiable White and Black gangs in prisons: Aryan Brotherhood, Skinheads, Bloods, and Crips. Report assesses strategies for controlling these potentially volatile special populations and identifies research needs.

Anti-Defamation League of B'nai B'rith. (1995). The Skinhead international: A worldwide survey of Neo-Nazi Skinheads. New York: Anti-Defamation League.

Eighteen-month study of the international Neo-Nazi Skinhead phenomenon. Based upon data collected from human rights organizations, law enforcement agencies, university-based research centers, and defectors. Article reports that the Skinhead movement is active in 33 countries, across 6 continents. Skinheads are found in the greatest numbers in Germany (5,000), Hungary and the Czech Republic (more than 4,000 each), the U.S. (3,500), Poland (2,000), the United Kingdom and Brazil (1,500 each), Italy (1,000 to 1,500), and Sweden (over 1,000).

Austin, Gregory A., & H. Lee. (1989). Substance abuse among Asian American youth. Washington, DC: U.S. Department of Education.

Report addresses extent of substance abuse among Asian American youth. While research has traditionally found that these youth use and abuse drugs significantly less than all other groups, recent evidence shows that the problem may be greater than what has been portrayed. Authors discuss how true levels of use may be masked by a tendency of the Asian American community to handle such problems within the family, rather than seek outside help.

Bryce, Herrington J. (Ed.). (1977). Black crime - A police view. Rockville, MD: National Institute of Justice.

Special anthology of papers presented at a conference sponsored by the L.E.A.A., Police Foundation, and the Joint Center for Political Studies. Discussants address the prevalence of Blacks in law enforcement, as well as rates of criminal offending. Specific topics include: role of crime in the political arena; police as causes of crime; power of police-community relations; and recruitment of African Americans by law enforcement agencies. Anthology concludes with discussion of how to reduce and control crime, as well as ways to improve police-community relations.

Bureau of Justice Assistance. (1997). A policy maker's guide to hate crimes. Washington, DC: U.S. Government Printing Office.

Monograph reviews recent literature on hate crimes, includes interviews with hate crime experts, and provides an overview of congressional hearings on hate crimes and terrorism. Overview of the scope and nature of America's hate crimes by local, state, and federal government agencies, law enforcement authorities, and civil rights groups. Research indicates African Americans are the most likely victims. Between 1991 to 1993, there were rising rates of Blacks charged with hate crime offenses, against Whites, Hispanics, and Asians.

Bureau of Justice Statistics. (1980). Capital punishment: 1979. Washington, DC: U.S. Government Printing Office.

Examines capital punishment in 1979. Data drawn from the National Prisoner Statistics program which includes inmates under sentence of death in 1979, on executions carried out from 1930 to 1979, and on recent trends in the evolution of capital punishment laws in the United States. From 1930 through 1979, 54 percent of the inmates executed were Black, 45 percent were White, and 1 percent were members of other races. The majority of executions were for murder, with Blacks accounting for 49 percent of the total executed for that crime. While only 12 percent of executions were for rape, approximately 90 of all prisoners executed for that crime were Black.

Bureau of Justice Statistics. (1990). Hispanic victims. Washington, DC: U.S. Government Printing Office.

Summary presents data on Hispanic victimization based on National Crime Victimization Survey. Findings are from bi-annual survey of 50,000 U.S. households conducted between 1979-1986. Among findings, Hispanics faced higher rates of victimization for violent and household crime (burglary, larceny, auto theft) than non-Hispanics; annual rates of crime by Hispanics dropped after 1983; Hispanic victims of violent crime were more likely to be accosted by a stranger than White or Black victims; and Hispanics are as likely as Blacks and Whites to report crime to the police.

Bureau of Justice Statistics. (1994). The costs of crime to victims: Crime data brief. Washington, DC: U.S. Government Printing Office.

Overview of 1992 data on economic costs associated with criminal victimization. For personal crimes, 11 percent of Whites and 15 percent of Blacks lose $500 or more. For household crimes, 23 percent of Whites and 25 percent of Blacks have such losses. In robberies, at least $250 is taken from the victim in about 26 percent of all victimizations. Of this percentage, White robbery victims constitute 19 percent and Blacks 41 percent. For lost time from work for personal crimes, 43 percent of Whites lose work compared with 67 percent of Blacks.

Bureau of Justice Statistics. (1995). Weapons offenses and offenders: Firearms, crime and criminal justice. Washington, DC: U.S. Government Printing Office.

Presents 1993 data on weapon offenses and offenders. Of those persons arrested by State and local agencies for weapons offenses in 1993, 92 percent were males, 77 percent were age 18 or older. Racial breakdown indicates that 55 percent were White, 43 percent were Black, 1 percent were Asians, and less than one percent were American Indian or Alaskan Native. Rates of arrest for weapons offenses (per 100,000) were 70, 362, and 40 for Whites, Blacks, and Other, respectively.

Bureau of Justice Statistics. (1996). Child victimizers: Violent offenders and their victims - Executive summary.

Washington, DC: U.S. Government Printing Office.

Executive summary reports the demographic characteristics of child victimizers and their victims. Among imprisoned violent offenders, approximately one-half are White and the other half are Black. A look at ethnicity indicates that approximately 14 percent of offenders are Hispanics. Data reveal that 70 percent of child victimizers are White, while about 25 percent are Black. The characteristics of child victims are as follows: 72 percent White; 24.5 percent Black; and 4 percent Other. Hispanic child victims comprise approximately 10 percent.

Bureau of Justice Statistics. (1997). Criminal victimization 1996: Changes 1995-96 with trends 1993-1996. Washington, DC: U.S. Government Printing Office.

Reports results of the National Crime Victimization Survey of 1996. Includes victimization data for Blacks and Whites and ethnicity (Hispanics and non-Hispanics). Survey indicates victimizations per 1,000 persons age 12 or older are as follows: 41 percent for Whites, 52.3 percent for Blacks, and 33.2 percent for Other races. For Hispanics and non-Hispanics, the rates are 44 percent for Hispanics and 42 percent for non-Hispanics. Statistics for murder and non-negligent manslaughter and household property crime victimization are also provided.

Bureau of Justice Statistics. (1997). Lifetime likelihood of going to state or federal prison. Washington, DC: U.S. Government Printing Office.

Report discusses the likelihood of Black, White, and Hispanic males and females going to state or Federal prison. Among men, Blacks (28.5 percent) are about twice as likely as Hispanics (16 percent) and six times more likely than Whites (4.4 percent) to be admitted to prison during their life. For women, the percentage estimates that they will enter prison at least once are 4 percent for Blacks, 1.5 percent for Hispanics, and less than one percent for Whites.

Bureau of Justice Statistics. (1997). Sex offenses and offenders: An analysis of data on rape and sexual assault. Washington, DC: U.S. Government Printing Office.

Report examines statistical databases maintained by both Bureau of Justice Statistics and Uniform Crime Reporting Program of the F.B.I. Provides comprehensive overview of incidence and prevalence of violent victimization by sexual assault in the U.S. between 1980 and 1995. For rape, 56 percent of arrestees were White, 42 percent were Black and 2 percent were of another race. In approximately 88 percent of rapes, victim and offender were of the same race. Black-on-Black rapes were two times more likely to involve the use of a gun or knife than White-on-White rapes. Black-on-White or White-on-Black sexual assaults were found equally likely to involve the use of a weapon.

Bureau of Justice Statistics. (1998). Capital punishment 1997. Washington, DC: U.S. Government Printing Office.

Overview of 1997 death row statistics for the United States. By year-end 1997, there were 3,335 prisoners on death row. The states with the largest death row populations are California (486), Texas (438), and Florida (370). Whites comprise the majority of persons on death row (1,876), followed by Blacks (1,406), American Indians (28), Asian Americans (17), and Other (8). Report includes other data on race, sex, and education levels of prisoners serving a sentence of death; what qualifies as a capital offense in states which have capital punishment; methods of execution; minimum age at which death penalty can be imposed in each state; and number of executions since the death penalty was re-instituted in 1976.

Bureau of Justice Statistics. (1998). Juvenile felony defendants in criminal courts: State court processing statistics, 1990-1994. Washington, DC: U.S. Government Printing Office.

Report provides statistical information on state criminal court processing of juvenile felony defendants between 1990 and 1994. In the nation's 75 largest counties, approximately 1 percent of all felony defendants were juveniles who were processed as adults in criminal courts. Of those juveniles transferred to the adult system, 63 percent were Black males, 29 percent were White males, 3 percent were Black females, and 2 percent were White females. White juveniles were responsible for 25 percent of violent crimes, 23 crimes of public order offenses, and 19 percent of drug-crimes. Black youths were responsible for 73 percent of violent offenses, 77 percent of public order offenses, and 81 percent of drug crimes. This racial pattern was reversed for property crimes where White youths were responsible for 63 percent and Black youths 31 percent.

Bureau of Justice Statistics. (1998). Police use of force: Collection of national data. Washington, DC: U.S. Government Printing Office.

Report on the 1996 Police-Public Contact Survey. Based on a nationally representative sample of 6,421 persons, 12 and older. Findings include 21 percent of population had face-to-face contact with police in 1996; men, Whites, and people in their twenties were most likely to have had contact with police; Hispanics and Blacks were about 70 percent as likely as Whites to have had contact with police; and men, minorities, and people under age 30 made up large percentage of those handcuffed in encounters with police.

Bureau of Justice Statistics. (1998). Prisoners in 1997. Washington, DC: U.S. Government Printing Office.

Report presents statistics for the number of inmates sentenced to federal and state prisons in 1997. By the end of 1997, the total number of adult prisoners under state and federal correctional supervision was 1.2 milliion. By midyear 1997, more than 1.7 million residents were either in jail or prison. Between 1990 and 1996, prisoners with sentences more than one year rose by more than 396,800 (54 percent). The number of White males increased by 46 percent, Black males 55 percent, White females 67 percent, and Black females 72 percent. At the end of 1996, there were more Black males in state and federal prisons (528,200) than White males (510,900).

Bureau of Justice Statistics. (1999). American Indians and crime. Washington, DC: U.S. Government Printing Office.

Comprehensive report of effects, consequences, and causes of violent crime involving American Indians. Data from B.J.S., F.B.I., and Bureau of the Census. Among the findings, American Indians have the highest victimization rate of any racial group; are more likely than other racial groups to be victims of interracial crime; are more likely to be victimized by someone who has consumed alcohol; and on any given day, 4 percent of American Indians over 18 are under criminal justice system jurisdiction.

Debro, Julius, & Helen Taylor. (1978). Study on the status of Black criminology in the United States. Rockville, MD: National Institute of Justice.

Report provides overview of works published by Black criminologists from 1875 to the 1970s, as well as studies conducted on Black crime by White authors between 1913-1978. Authors note how perceptions of justice among Blacks have consistently differed from those held by Whites. Additionally, they address the changing nature of Black crime over the past 100 years -- the nonviolent offenses Blacks living in the South were routinely accused of to an increase in violent crimes more typical of urban living.

Donziger, Steven R. (1996). The real war on crime: The report of the National Criminal Justice Commission. New York: HarperPerennial.

Report on crime and criminal justice processing from cross-section of U.S. The Commission was comprised of educators, community leaders, academics, athletes, and policy makers. Various topics explored, such as fear of crime and its impact on policy; racial bias in War on Drug's policy approach; and the rise of the prison industrial complex. Report concludes with eleven policy recommendations, including requiring a racial impact statement before implementation of any major crime policies, and imposition of a three-year moratorium on prison construction.

Farber, William O., Phillip A. Odeen, & Robert A. Tschetter. (1957). Indians, law enforcement and local government - A study of the impact of the off-reservation Indian problem on South Dakota local government with special reference to law enforcement. Vermillion, SD: University of South Dakota - Institute of Indian Studies.

Report addresses the challenges brought about by the increased migration of Native American populations from the reservation to urban centers, particularly for local law enforcement. Interviews were conducted with local officials and citizens, as well as federal and state officials involved in Indian Affairs. Cultural differences and poor job skills have hampered the assimilation of Indians into the economic base in rural communities. Consequently, such communities have witnessed an escalation of crime among the Native populations. Report addresses the impact this increase has had on local resources and recommends an increase in federal aid for commuity programs to aid the successful transition of indigenous persons into these communities.

French, Laurence (Ed.). (1982). Indians and criminal justice. Rockville, MD: National Institute of Justice.

Edited volume on American Indians is organized around the following topics: socio-legal issues applicable to Native Americans; Indian crime and justice and, treatment concerns in dealing with indigenous populations. Essays address critical legal issues applicable to Native populations; basics of American Indian law; patterns and theories of Indian crime; and specialized Indian correctional treatment.

Independent Commission on the Los Angeles Police Department. (1991). Report of the Independent Commission on the Los Angeles Police Department: Summary. Los Angeles: Author.

This study, also known as the Christopher Commission Report, was initiated by the April 1991 videotaped beating of Rodney King. Examines the extent to which the L.A.P.D. has used excessive force. The investigation revealed that a significant number of officers repeatedly ignore the department's written policies and guidelines on the use of force. Report finds that lack of supervision, management inattention to police abuses, and the department's emphasis on aggressive crime control, exacerbated existing problems. Commission recommends a two-term limit for police chiefs and increase sanctions against police abuse and racial bias.

Los Angeles, CA Board of Police Commissioners. (1996). In the course of change: The Los Angeles Police Department five years after the Christopher Commission. Los Angeles: Los Angeles Police Department.

Official report outlines the progress achieved by the L.A.P.D. since the Rodney King racial conflicts, as measured by both the structural and cultural framework changes suggested by the Christopher Commission in 1991. Report concludes that although significant progress has been made in the development of a police-community partnership, the department has only made halting progress in attaining management accountability for dealing with at-risk officers.

Mauer, Marc. (1990). <u>Young Black men and the criminal justice system: A growing national problem</u>. Washington, DC: Sentencing Project.

Report on the state of young Black men invovled in the criminal justice system. Report reviews 1989 data for Whites, Blacks and Hispanics, between ages 20-29. Findings indicate that almost one-third of all young Black men are either on probation, parole, or incarcerated. For young White men, the figure is 6.2 percent and for young Hispanic men, the figure is 10.4 percent. Though the percentages are much lower, young females follow the same pattern as their male counterparts; 2.7 percent (Black females), 1.0 (White females) and 1.8 (Hispanic females). Report concludes that these disproportionately high figures for Black men will have a detrimental impact on the Black community; indicate that the War on Drugs has failed and signal the need to re-design the criminal justice policy.

Mauer, Marc. (1997). <u>Intended and unintended consequences: State racial disparities in imprisonment</u>. Washington, DC: The Sentencing Project.

Data from 38 states and the District of Columbia, between 1988 and 1994. Report analyzes rates of incarceration by race. Particularly, the impact current sentencing policies have had on the African American community. Findings indicate that over this time period, the Black rate of incarceration in state prisons increased from 7 to 8 times the White rate. Report also presents data on the sociological consequences of incarceration trends, including high rates of disenfranchisement for Black men.

Mauer, Marc, & Tracy Huling. (1995). <u>Young Black Americans</u>

and the criminal justice system: Five years later. Washington,
DC: The Sentencing Project.

Report updates information from the 1990 Sentencing Project
Report on young Black Americans and the criminal justice
system. The report outlines criminal justice control rates in the
1990s for Blacks, Hispanics, and Whites; the
overrepresentation of young Black males in the criminal justice
system; the impact of the War on Drugs on Blacks and
Hispanics; increasing criminal justice control rates for women;
and other important sentencing topics. Report also notes the
increasing control rates for minority women. Mauer and
Huling conclude with several policy recommendations,
including a reduction in the number of low-level drug arrests.

Milne, J. W., & R. W. Johnson. (1980). Criminal law for Indian
courts. Rockville, MD: National Institute of Justice.

Detailed report on criminal law as it applies to American
Indian tribal justice system. Attention is directed to the
challenges inherent in a multi-jurisdictional approach that has
been adopted in the handling of Indian criminal and civil
matters. Authors provide a series of charts to illustrate the
various jurisdictions. Special section is dedicated to a detailed
discussion of juvenile justice within the tribal court system and
the Indian Child Welfare Act.

Moynihan, Daniel P. (1965). The Negro family: The case for national
action. Washington, DC: The Office of Planning and
Research, U.S. Department of Labor.

Controversial report explores range of issues relating to the
Black family. Study looks at a wide-range of factors, including
slavery, reconstruction, urbanization, unemployment, female-
headed households, crime and alienation. Report finds
disproportionately high rates of offending and victimization for
Blacks and how these are interrelated with other variables,

such as family structure.

Myers, Samuel L. (1980). Blacks and crime - Economic theories and realities. Rockville, MD: National Institute of Justice.

Report examines correlation between Black disproportionate involvement in the criminal justice system and racial disparities in employment. Author discusses the current nature of the Black labor market, one characterized by substandard wages, menial occupations, and high rates of unemployment and turnover. Consequently, crime may provide more economic potential for Blacks than it would for Whites. The situation is made even more complex for Black ex-offenders seeking legitimate employment opportunities. Author suggests the adoption of wage subsidy programs to encourage employers to provide more economic opportunities for this population.

Myers, Samuel L. (1981). Racism and the criminal justice system. Rockville, MD: National Institute of Justice.

Report draws from state prison data to explore reasons for the disproportionate involvement of Blacks in the criminal justice system. Author argues contemporary incarceration rates are a reflection of historical patterns of racism and slavery in the United States. To explain recidivism rates found among Black offenders, author tests the hypothesis that participation in crime is a consequence of constrained economic opportunities within the African American community. Findings reveal that differences in recidivism can be rectified when employment opportunities are more equitably distributed across all racial and ethnic populations.

National American Indian Court Judges Association. (1978). Indian courts and the future - Report of the NAICJA (National American Indian Court Judges Association) long range planning project. Washington, DC: U.S. Department of the

Interior, Bureau of Indian Affairs.

Report on findings by the National American Indian Court Judges Association (NAICJA) on ways to improve the current tribal court system. Background information on court operations was gathered through site visits to 23 Indian Courts across the nation. Report first addresses the historical basis for tribal courts, then directs its attention to the current state of the tribal court system. Report concludes with a five year plan to improve current operations. Suggestions include: additional tribal legislation, increased facilities and equipment, and commuity relations and education.

National Institute for Juvenile Justice and Delinquency Prevention. (1980). A preliminary national assessment of the numbers and characteristics of juveniles processed in the juvenile justice system. Washington, DC: U.S. Government Printing Office.

Study examines the number and characteristics of persons under 18 processed throughout the United States by the official juvenile justice system for 1977. Data were drawn from the Uniform Crime Reports, Uniform Parole Reports, children in custody, and the National Center for Juvenile Justice. Estimated 2,508,961 persons under the age of 8 were arrested or referred to the juvenile justice system in 1977. Intake decision to file for court action was related to race in that there was a slight tendency to file cases involving Blacks more often than those involving Whites or other races.

National Institute of Justice. (1992). Native American delinquency: An overview of prevalence, causes and correlates, and promising tradition-based approaches to sanctioning. Washington, DC: U.S. Government Printing Office.

Reviewing the existing body of knowledge about Native American delinquency, this government document looks at issues of juvenile justice and delinquency. In particular, a review of Native American justice and federal jurisdiction notes that the basic concern which continues to be raised and redefined is which level of government -- tribal, state, or Federal--should assume jurisdiction over particular kinds and categories of misconduct.

National Institute of Justice. (1996). The new immigrant Hispanic population: An integrated approach to preventing delinquency and crime. Washington, DC: U.S. Government Printing Office.

Summary of presentation about research on Puerto Rican adolescent males in New York. Publication reports that traditional Hispanic family culture appears to deter delinquency. Acculturation is associated with delinquency, and adolescents not in the labor force are less likely to become involved in crime than those who hold jobs. New theoretical frameworks are needed to explain Hispanic juvenile delinquency. A useful integrative approach would include socio-economic, psychosocial, and social science theories.

National Institute of Justice. (1997). Crack, powder cocaine, and heroin: Drug purchase and use patterns in six U.S. cities. Washington, DC: U.S. Government Printing Office.

Report presents information collected from 2,056 recently arrested powder cocaine, crack cocaine, and heroin users from Chicago, Manhattan, Portland, San Antonio, San Diego, and Washington. Data on where and how arrestee obtained drugs. Report indicates that White and Hispanic users spread their drug use relatively evenly across powder, crack, and heroin, while Black drug arrestee primarily use crack. For most drug users in most cities, Whites are more likely than Blacks to report purchasing their supply from a single source. Findings reveal that the powder, crack, and heroin markets are substantially different from one another.

National Institute of Justice. (1997). Guns in America: National
    survey on private owners. Washington, DC: U.S. Government
    Printing Office.

Brief reports the results of a nationally representative
telephone survey (1994) on the use of firearms and private
ownership by American adults. Whites are substantially more
likely to own guns than Blacks (27 versus 16 percent), and
Blacks are more likely than Hispanics (16 versus 11 percent).
For handguns alone, however, the ownership rates among
Blacks and Whites are nearly equal (13 versus 16 percent).
Gun ownership is highest among middle-aged, college-
educated people living in rural areas and small towns.

National Minority Advisory Council on Criminal Justice. (1982).
    Inequality of justice - A report on crime and the adminstration
    of justice in the minority community. Rockville, MD:
    National Institute of Justice.

Report examines the role race plays in the operation of the
United States criminal justice system. Authors note that while
minorities are more likely than Whites to be victims of and
perpetrators of crime, their cases are often delegated to non-
minority, inexperienced, or incompetent criminal justice
personnel. The problem is further compounded by the lack of
bilingual and cultural diversity training for court personnel.
Findings are based on relevant literature, public hearings, and
field studies, as well as interviews with minority leaders and
public officials. Authors recommend the creation of a national
database on the current status of ethnic and racial minorities in
the criminal justice sytem, as well as the multi-cultural training
of all court personnel.

National Organization for Victims. (1992). Responding to
    Hispanic victims of crime: A training course for victim service
    providers. Washington, DC: U.S. Government Printing Office.

Provides a course outline designed to teach crime victim service providers techniques in responding to Hispanic victims of crime. Manual compiled by the U.S. Office for Victims of Crime. Includes descriptions of Hispanic cultural attitudes, values, beliefs, and concepts that may be useful in working with Hispanic populations. Text is divided into three sections: training techniques, lectures and exercises, and suggested readings.

Office of Juvenile Justice and Delinquency Prevention. (1998). Disproportionate minority confinement: 1997 update. Washington, DC: U.S. Government Printing Office.

Overview of juvenile minority confinement and congressional legislation enacted to combat this problem. Minority juveniles constitute 32 percent of the youth population, yet they are 68 percent of the confined juvenile population. In 1988 Congress passed amendments to the Juvenile Justice and Delinquency Prevention Act. These additions require states to address minority confinement in their funding requests and tie future eligibility to compliance. Report outlines O.J.J.D.P. strategies, indicates the degree to which each state is in compliance with mandate, and offers successful state models used to address disproportionate minority confinement.

Office of Juvenile Justice and Delinquency Prevention. (1998). Highlights of the 1996 national youth gang survey. Washington, DC: U.S. Government Printing Office.

Fact sheet reports highlights of the 1996 National Youth Gang Survey. Sample includes information from 1,216 police departments of large cities, 664 suburban police and county sheriff's departments, 399 police departments of small cities, and 745 rural police and county sheriff's departments. Hate gangs, motorcycle gangs, prison gangs, and exclusively adult gangs were excluded from the survey. Of the gang members, 44 percent were Hispanic, 35 percent Black, 14 percent White,

5 percent Asian, and 2 percent Other race. Notably, the proportion of White gang members in rural counties (32 percent) and small cities (31 percent) was more than twice the national average. Although Hispanics and Blacks continued to comprise most of the gang members, almost one-third of the gang members in small cities and rural counties were White.

Office of Juvenile Justice and Delinquency Prevention. (1998). Juvenile court statistics 1995. Washington, DC: U.S. Government Printing Office.

Description of the delinquency and status offense cases handled by the U.S. juvenile courts in 1995. White youths accounted for 66 percent of the delinquency cases disposed by juvenile courts. White youths were responsible for 58 percent of person offense cases, 70 percent of property offense cases, 64 percent of drug violations, 64 percent of public order cases. Black youths were responsible for 31 percent of all delinquency cases, 38 percent of person offense cases, 26 percent of property cases, 34 percent of drug cases, and 33 percent of public order cases.

Rider, Anthony O. (1980). The firesetter: A psychological profile. F.B.I. Law Enforcement Bulletin, Washington D.C., 49 (6,7,8,), 5-11, 6-13, 16-17.

Explores arson and the psychological profile of arsonists. Arsonists, those psychologically motivated to set fires, are typically 25 years old, White, and male. They have a history of poor academic performance, unstable families, criminal involvement, and difficulties in social relationships. Arsonists tend to lack self-confidence, self-control and, experience significant stress and sadistic-aggressive tendencies. In contrast, the hired arsonist tends to be a White male between the ages of 30 and 50 with above average intelligence. These arsonists rely on manipulation, deceit, and exploitation to carry out their crimes.

Swan, L. Alex. (1982). Incarceration rates - Blacker than White.
    Rockville, MD: National Institute of Justice.

    Report examines the disproportionate incarceration rates of
    Blacks compared to those of Whites. Author argues such
    patterns are not a reflection of a disproportionate involvement
    in crime by African-Americans, rather it is a reflection of
    criminal justice policies that focus on street crime.
    Consequently, such decisions have bolstered the misperception
    that Blacks are criminogenic by nature. Swan argues that
    racial discrimination in the criminal justice system will cease
    only when a shift occurs in the dominant political and social
    institutions.

Thurston, Linda M. (Ed.). (1993). A call to action: An analysis
    and overview of the United States criminal justice system, with
    recommendations. Chicago: Third World Press.

    Report of the National Commission on Crime and Justice.
    This commission, solely comprised of minority members,
    examines current state of criminal justice system. Evaluation
    is based upon broad review of the literature, as well as a series
    of public hearings. Findings reveal that minorities are
    disproportionately over represented at all stages of the criminal
    justice system. Recommendations include further
    development of community-based programs, reduced reliance
    on imprisonment for crime control, and increased support of
    individual and community responsibility for crime prevention
    and control.

U.S. Department of Health and Human Services. (1997). National
    Household Survey on Drug Abuse: Population estimates 1996.
    Rockville, MD: SAMHSA/OAS.

    Detailed, comprehensive look at the prevalence of drug use in
    the U.S. Data provided on White, Hispanic, and Black drug
    use including illicit drugs (e.g., marijuana, cocaine, heroin),

alcohol, tobacco products, and nonmedical use of prescription drugs. Beyond race, survey includes data on region, age, and sex. Survey based on stratified, multi-stage probability sample. Findings based upon interviews with 18,269 U.S. residents.

U.S. National Criminal Justice Information and Statistics Service. (1979). Criminal victimization in the United States: 1977. A national crime survey report. Washington, DC: U.S. Government Printing Office.

National survey of 1977 victimization of persons age 12 and over. These crimes include burglary, larceny, rape, robbery, assault, and motor vehicle theft. Sample includes 136,000 occupants of 60,000 households representative of all households in the United States. The incidence of personal crimes of rape, robbery, and all assault were relatively higher among males, younger persons, Blacks, Hispanics, divorced or seperated persons, the poor, the unemployed, and city residents. Blacks had higher victimization rates than Whites for household burglary or motor vehicle theft.

U.S. National Criminal Justice Information and Statistics Service. (1979). Rape victimization in 26 American cities. Washington, DC: U.S. Government Printing Office.

Rape and attempted rape in 26 cities of the U.S. as part of 1974 National Crime Survey was examined. Survey included 10,000 households (22,000 persons) in 1974-1975. Survey also examined characteristics of the offenders as perceived by their victims. Approximately 39,310 rapes and attempted rapes occurred in 26 cities. There were higher rates of rape and attempted rape for Black and other minority women compared to White women.

Western Regional Conference on 'Just Us' - Young Pan Asian females and the juvenile justice system - Proceedings, October 18,

1980, Seattle, Washington. (1980). Rockville, MD: National
Institute of Justice.

Review of papers presented at a conference on the prevalence
and causes of delinquency among Asian American females.
Panelists covered a multitude of Asian Pacific cultures
including Chinese, Japanese, Korean, and Vietnamese.
Prevalence of delinquency among this specific population may
be attributed to the rigid values and gender roles projected in
such cultures.   Contributors addressed some of the social
challenges facing Asian American females -- such as,
assimilation, alienation, and familial estrangement. To counter
this growing problem authors present a number of
recommendations: increased availability of bilingual
counselors in local school systems, mentoring programs
specially developed for females, and the development of a
national database on Asian American female delinquents.

Woods, R. G., & A. M. Harkins. (1970). Rural and city Indians in
    Minnesota prisons. Arlington, VA: U.S. Department of
    Health, Education, and Welfare.

Report analyzes data of court commitments of Indian offenders
in Minnesotta's correctional system. Discussion addresses
how assimilation efforts for Indian youth can be improved,
both within and outside the correctional system. Authors
recommend greater attention be paid to cultural attitudes
Native Americans have towards the concept of law, as well as
property. Report concludes with recommendation to adopt an
adapted version of Project Newgate, a program that uses higher
education as a means to rehabilitation.

III

ELECTRONIC RESOURCES

Part 9

Websites

Bureau of Justice Statistics
http://www.ojp.usdoj.gov/bjs/

Categorized by topic, site provides basic statistical information on criminal justice in the United States. Topics include: drugs and crime; law enforcement; prosecution and sentencing; and corrections.

Cecil Greek's Criminal Justice Webpage: Florida State University School of Criminology
http://www.criminology.fsu.edu/cj.html

Comprehensive website, which provides numerous criminal justice related links. Sample of categories include: Federal criminal justice agencies, international criminal justice sources, crime and crime prevention, juvenile delinquency and juvenile justice, and drug and alcohol information.

Death Penalty Information Center
http://www.essential.org/dpic/

Provides analysis and information on issues surrounding the death penalty. Links user to publications on the cost, racial disparities, and trends in capital punishment.

National Archive of Criminal Justice Data
http://www.icpsr.umich.edu/NACJD/

Sponsored by a number of national government agencies,
archive is categorized by subject and allows for keyword
searches. Topics include: Police, courts, corrections, the
criminal justice system, and crime and delinquency. Links also
allow access to a number of other university departments for
searches within conjoining archives of political and social
research.

National Criminal Justice Reference Services
http://www.ncjrs.org/

Operated by NCJRS, the Justice Information Center provides
links to topical categories in criminal justice, as well as access
to the NCJRS Abstracts database. Also serves as link to
various federal agencies, such as: U.S. Department of Justice,
National Institute of Justice, Office of Juvenile Justice and
Delinquency Prevention, and the Office of National Drug
Control Policy.

National Household Survey on Drug Abuse
http://www.samhsa.gov
http://www.health.org

Data provided on White, Hispanic, and Black drug use
including illicit drugs (e.g., marijuana, cocaine, heroin),
alcohol, tobacco products, and nonmedical use of prescription
drugs. Beyond race, survey includes data on region, age, and
sex. Survey based on stratified, multi-stage probability
sample.

Sourcebook of Criminal Justice Statistics
http://www.albany.edu/sourcebook/

Online site for the annual Sourcebook of Criminal Justice

Statistics, published by the Bureau of Justice Statistics. Users may receive both updates on the Sourcebook, as well as browse by topical category or keyword.

U.S. Sentencing Commission
http://www.ussc.gov/

Provides information about the U.S. Sentencing Commission and tracks its activities. In addition, links user with publication lists available through organization on sentencing statistics and commissions by state.

Author Index

All authors names which appear in bibliography as either author, co-author, or named contributor are included below.

Lynch, Michael, 142, 143.
Ma, Yue, 33.
Macallair, Dan, 87.
MacCoun, Robert, 70.
MacLean, Brian, 142.
Maclin, Tracey, 66.
Mann, Coramae, 111, 138, 143, 149.
Marshall, Thurgood, 150.
Martin, Susan, 111.
Martinez, Ramiro, 43, 44, 143.
Massey, Douglas, 111.
Matthews, Catherine, xi.
Mauer, Marc, 66, 162.
Maupin, James, 39.
Maxwell, Jane, 40.
Mazzella, Ronald, 112.
McCain, Tracey, 66.
McCall, Patricia, 49, 115.
McClain, Paula, 71.
McCord, Joan, 138, 143.
McDermid, Lea, 87.
McDermott, Joan, 64.
McIntyre, Charshee, 67.
McKee, James, 67.
McMorris, Barbara, 116.
Meares, Tracey, 68.
Megargee, Edwin, 92.
Melton, Ada, 22.
Mercy, James, 113.
Meroy, John, 7.
Messerschmidt, James, 112.
Meyer, J'ona, 21, 113.
Meyers, John, 7.
Michels, Jennifer, 5.
Miller, Jerome, 68, 149.
Miller, Steven, 47.
Miller, Walter, 8.
Milne, J. W., 163.
Milovanovic, Dragan, 142, 146.
Minnis, Mhyra, 21.
Mirande, Alfredo, 44, 141.
Moffitt, Terrie, 144.
Monikowski, Richard, 22.
Monk, Richard, 147.

Moore, Jack, 8.
Morris, Norval, 103.
Morris, Thomas, 136.
Motley, Constance Baker, 74.
Moynihan, Daniel, 163.
Murray, Charles, 100, 140.
Murty, Komanduri, 10, 116.
Myers, Laura, 138.
Myers, Martha, 136, 138.
Myers, Samuel, 113, 144, 164.
Myrdal, Gunnar, 126
Nalla, Mahesh, 142.
Nelson, Caroline, 5.
Nelson, Margaret, 122.
Nielson, Marianne, 22.
Nordquist, Joan, x, 144.
O'Carroll, Patrick, 113.
O'Day, Patrick, 107.
Odeen, Phillip, 160.
Oetting, E. R., 86.
Ogawa, Brian, 114.
O'Keefe, Maura, 114.
Oli, Sampson, 148.
Oliver, Mary, 115.
Oliver, William, 68.
Owens, Charles, 137, 144.
Parker, Karen, 115.
Parker, Keith, 116.
Patenaude, Allan, 148.
Paternoster, Ray, 22.
Patterson, E. Britt, 142.
Patterson, James, 69.
Peak, Ken, 22, 69.
Pecos Melton, Ada, 22.
Peeples, Faith, 116.
Peffley, Mark, 7, 9.
Peller, Gary, 116.
Pena, Albert, 24.
Pendergrast, Robert, 54.
Pendleton, Michael, 9.
Perry, Ronald, 117.
Petersilia, Joan, 106, 117.
Peterson, George, 138.
Peterson, Ruth, 97, 122.
Phillips, G.Howard, 9.

Subject Index

Under each of the primary subject headings, entries that specifically addressed the core racial/ethnic group(s) are listed first. Other sub-topics then follow in alphabetical order.

About the Compilers

KATHERYN K. RUSSELL is an Associate Professor in the Criminology and Criminal Justice Department at the University of Maryland, College Park.

HEATHER L. PFEIFER is a doctoral student in the Criminology and Criminal Justice Department at the University of Maryland, College Park.

JUDITH L. JONES is a doctoral student in the College of Criminal Justice at Sam Houston State University.

ISBN 0-313-31033-5

90000>

EAN

9 780313 310331

HARDCOVER BAR CODE